Retreats
to Retirement

Retreats
to Retirement

Dream Homes to Reality

E. Ashley Rooney

Foreword by Lavae Aldrich

4880 Lower Valley Road, Atglen, PA 19310 USA

Courtesy of ©Suki Coughlin/Paula McFarland Stylist

Front cover center: *Courtesy of Topsider;* top: *Courtesy of Juliet Jones Photofolio, Inc.*; bottom right: *Courtesy of Dan Tyrpak*; bottom left: *Courtesy of D. Peter Lund.*
Back cover top: *Courtesy of ©Suki Coughlin/Paula McFarland Stylist;* center: *Courtesy of Bob Greenspan*; bottom: *Courtesy of Sears Barrett.*
Spine photo: *Courtesy of John Canham.*

Copyright © 2005 by E. Ashley Rooney
Library of Congress Control Number: 2005930796

Designed by Mark David Bowyer
Type set in CopprplGoth Bd BT/Korinna BT

ISBN: 0-7643-2339-3
Printed in China

Published by Schiffer Publishing Ltd.
4880 Lower Valley Road
Atglen, PA 19310
Phone: (610) 593-1777; Fax: (610) 593-2002
E-mail: Info@schifferbooks.com

For the largest selection of fine reference books on this and related subjects, please visit our web site at
www.schifferbooks.com
We are always looking for people to write books on new and related subjects. If you have an idea for a book please contact us at the above address.

This book may be purchased from the publisher.
Include $3.95 for shipping.
Please try your bookstore first.
You may write for a free catalog.

In Europe, Schiffer books are distributed by
Bushwood Books
6 Marksbury Ave.
Kew Gardens
Surrey TW9 4JF England
Phone: 44 (0) 20 8392-8585; Fax: 44 (0) 20 8392-9876
E-mail: info@bushwoodbooks.co.uk
Free postage in the U.K., Europe; air mail at cost.

C O N T E N T S

Courtesy of Ron Rusico.

ACKNOWLEDGMENTS

Second home ownership has jumped significantly in the past ten years – primarily because the price is right and real estate is appreciating. Today, motivated by those same factors and some additional ones such as an erratic stock market and a desire to move closer to the children, more people are purchasing or building second and third homes.

An architect pointed out to me that while some vacation-to-retirement home buyers are motivated by profit possibilities, many are in it for the lifestyle.

Architects and builders assist people in translating their visions into reality – and people have many dreams about that vacation-to-retirement home.

A good designer will attempt to understand the way clients see their ideal home, clarifying both pragmatic considerations such as types and numbers of rooms and artistic matters related to reflecting the client's personality and way of life. The resulting plan fuses these interests and adapts them in form and space.

I worked with many excellent architects and designers in developing this book. As always, I learned many things such as what a "Truth Hole" is (see Scott Rodwin's house, page 119). I also met many homeowners who graciously permitted us to photograph their homes in Florida, New Hampshire, and Massachusetts.

Several people stood out. Cape Cod architect, Mark Farber, his family, and friends were key. They were great sources of wisdom about building vacation houses that would be ultimately be used as permanent residences. Lavae Aldrich from Aldrich Architects, Issaquah, Washington, wrote a charming essay about finding and building a house of their dreams. Charlene Keogh, the owner of Keogh Design Inc., provided detailed information about the collaboration that occurs between client and designer.

Then there are those fantastic photographers who are willing to share their creativity.

Finally, D. Peter Lund has remained a good friend throughout this process.

Facing page: *Courtesy of Ron Rusico.*

LATITUDE ADJUSTMENT

—Lavae Aldrich, Aldrich Architects
Issaquah, Washington

My husband and I had never really thought about retirement. But we found Costa Rica immediately enchanting on our first vacation there eight years ago. The very first day, ambling down the road in front of our six-room Caribbean hotel to the local eatery, I began to fantasize about a little cabin in the woods or a place on the beach. But I didn't mention anything to Steve for another week of traveling around. Towards the end of our trip, we were driving along in our rental car in the hills above the Pacific coast when he turned off the main road at a sign in a small village. The dirt road led to a sign that read *Lotes Se Vende.* It was immediately apparent that he was harboring his own fantasies.

For the next year we continued to share our dreams of a place by the water. We explored every salt-water cove and peek-a-boo view near our home in the Puget Sound region of Washington state. Two things stopped us from buying a lot that winter: the inapproachable costs of purchasing and developing our dream in one of the most expensive areas of the country and the fifty-degree temperature of the water. Having grown up in the Northwest, we both know well that it's a very hot summer day indeed that invites one to swim in water that can only be described as frigid. So we set our dreams aside and took another vacation to the tropics.

When we arrived in a particular little beach town, we began earnestly looking for property to buy. By then, we had seen most parts of this incredibly diverse little country: the humid Caribbean coast with its crystal turquoise waters and palm-line coves, the forested mountains of the Cordillera de Tilaran, the peaceful northern cattle lands of Guanacaste, the temperate mesa around the capital of San Jose, and the straight sunny beaches of northern Nicoya. On the southern face of the peninsula, this town was perfect: an exquisite, crescent-shaped, palm-lined beach sheltered by a coral reef, a nice little town with good restaurants frequently enjoyed by "Ticos" (as Costa Ricans call themselves) as well as foreign tourists, surrounded by green hills, and with an excellent hardware store.

We spent three days walking and surveying every lot with a respectable ocean view. Although there were lots available on the beach, we didn't consider them seriously because of the lease limitations, humidity, and our own need for privacy and solitude. We settled on a steep site in the hills just one-quarter mile from the beach, with clear title. The previous owner had already cut three separate building sites into the hillside. A well already drilled on site and further rights to public water and power in the road gave this lot a leg up compared with many of the others we explored. In the first of our many email negotiations around this house, we bought the property over the Internet from the seller in Italy.

Our first thoughts were simple. We'd build a utility structure housing plumbing, utilities, and storage, and surround it with pavilions for sleeping, lounging, and cooking. But over the next four years, as our stays in the

A tropical dream, Casa El Gecko is sited on a hill overlooking a crescent bay in Central America. The masonry structure is surrounded by a deep shaded veranda and sheltering roof. Strategically placed windows and doors capture fresh sea breezes, which flow easily through the open floor plan. Designed to blend the interior with the exterior in this nearly perfect climate, Casa El Gecko provides a frequent latitude adjustment while the working couple await retirement.

area became longer and more comfortable and our available funds increased, the dream grew. We spent as much time on the property as we could, in as many varied seasons as possible. We became clear about the extent and limits of our needs for comfort and accommodation. We found the best parts of the property. And we got to know the neighbors. But, because I had never been my own client before, the design process was difficult and emotional, yet ultimately rewarding.

The site we had found for our retirement dream was fabulous. The views are incredible, centered on a small island at the eastern end of the bay. We can watch the waves lapping the shore at low tide and hear the surf crashing on the reef. Looking east we see the forest-covered hills above the neighboring bay and the lighted soccer (football) field at the village down the road. The western view peeks around the precious shade of our bamboo to a headland and the setting sun. It all mandated that the house be positioned high on the hill to embrace the views, while also capturing the cooling breezes off the Pacific.

After talking to several builders, we determined to work with a local builder. A Tico project manager made weekly inspections for us, answering the contractor's questions and keeping track of our interests while we were 3000 miles away. During the yearlong construction process, he frequently emailed digital pictures to demonstrate progress and review detail questions. I visited the building site once, to inspect the progress and deliver hardware and finish materials purchased in the United States.

The peaceful natural surroundings drove us to blend the inside and the outside in the traditional Tico style. A deep veranda wraps around two sides of the house and expands to a large terrace where most of the living occurs. The interior core is an open plan with sitting area and kitchen. The wall between disappears with the folding of solid teak doors that stack against a wall. Birds and monkeys are ever present. Their songs and calls provide the soundtrack of life at Casa El Gecko.

Most of the living occurs on the terrace.

Keeping the floor plan open, for maximum flexibility and free airflow, the combination guest quarters and den occupy an alcove. Bright silk curtains can be pulled at night, leaving the breezes free flowing or if guests need more privacy, the teak accordion door stretches across the arch. The adjacent bathroom opens onto the garden with a small hand sink. Most of the bathing is done al fresco, in the outdoor shower facing Punta Samara.

A large peninsula encloses the kitchen, which is great for spreading a tropical buffet or chatting up the cook. Because vacations often include extended family and friends, the kitchen workspace is ample enough for several cooks.

Upstairs, the master bedroom has its own covered terrace, large enough for serving group cocktails at sunset, working on the laptop, or curling up with a good read. A long desk within the bedroom is ample for two. The adjacent powder room has its own view. Filtering through the bougainvillea up the hill, fresh breezes sweep across the custom-designed bed made from tropical hardwood.

Doors and windows are positioned throughout the house for maximum ventilation. High ceilings and paddle fans keep the moist Pacific air moving throughout the house. The masonry structure absorbs the sun's heat and cools the house another ten degrees. At eight degrees latitude, there is no need for a furnace or even glass in the windows. Simple wood framed screens open on hinges, and solid teak shutters provide security. Narrow screened louvers above the windows and doors maintain ventilation, even when the house is closed, sometimes for several months at a time, eliminating any chance of mustiness or mildew.

Completed just a year ago, we vacation here as often as we can. Our intentions to retire in tropical peace are strengthened each time we visit. Living at Casa El Gecko is relaxing, spiritually refreshing, and reorienting.

We call it our latitude adjustment. The Ticos call it *pura vida* or pure life. My brother adds, *pura vida facial.*

We designed the house using the traditional local construction system. Concrete block walls are topped with a wood-framed roof and covered with sheet metal roofing. Although most roofs in Costa Rica are red, reminiscent of clay tile, we chose a green metal to blend in against the verdant hillside. A wide roof with deep overhangs shelters the house and its inhabitants from scorching sun and, at times, torrential rains. We collect the rainwater from the roof and recycle it for irrigation, showers, and a future plunge pool/ waterfall.

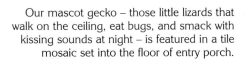
Our mascot gecko – those little lizards that walk on the ceiling, eat bugs, and smack with kissing sounds at night – is featured in a tile mosaic set into the floor of entry porch.

We designed the house to blend the inside and the outside in the traditional Tico style. A deep veranda and wide arches wrap around two sides and expand to a large covered terrace. This is where most of the daily living happens. The wall between the inside and the outside disappears when solid teak doors are folded and stacked against a wall. A sitting area and the kitchen, separated only by a large peninsula, are just inside the terrace.

The exterior doors and shutters are arched to mimic the stucco arches on the veranda. Interior doors are all louvered to enhance ventilation. The cabinets also have louvered doors to keep contents fresh. All the cabinet doors and drawers are fitted with locks, using a number of different key cylinders. This way we can offer renters their own lockable storage, keeping some precious items for ourselves, and the maid has her own stash of linens and supplies.

We are continually surrounded with beauty.

Although we find this climate and environment infinitely comfortable, it brings problems that must be addressed in design and construction. Because it is highly corrosive, we avoided the use of metals whenever possible. And when not possible to avoid, we used the best quality we could afford. All the door hardware and hinges are stainless steel.

Vacation-to-Retirement Homes

Vacation homes are a dream for many of us. They respond to our need for recreation and respite, revitalization and refuge. They range from large summer estates in Newport, Rhode Island, condos in Venice, Florida, or simple fishing cabins on Puget Sound.

The lure of a vacation property has persisted for centuries. English and French royalty had country homes where they would retire for recreation and rest. Nineteenth century millionaires during the Gilded Age in the United States built great summer cottages in Newport, upstate New York, and Maine, where they could retire in unabashed opulence for six weeks during the heat of the summer. Others built in Virginia's horse country, the piney woods of the Berkshires in Massachusetts, the rolling hills of Southeast Pennsylvania, and Florida, of course.

According to the experts, today's popular spots include:
- Cape Cod, Massachusetts
- Island Beach, New Jersey
- Cape May, New Jersey
- Lake Tahoe, California (El Dorado County)
- Boca Raton, Florida (Palm Beach County)
- Brigantine Island, New Jersey
- Gulf Coast, Florida
- Jupiter Island, Florida
- Punta Gorda, Florida
- Sanibel Island, Florida
- Berkshire Mountains, Massachusetts
- Naples, Florida
- Sedona, Arizona

Some go one step further: they buy a vacation home as an investment in the future – a possible place for retirement. The concept of buying or build-

Courtesy of D. Peter Lund.

ing a vacation-to-retirement home sparks our imaginations and allows us to dream of escaping our normal humdrum existence.

We see this home as a central gathering place, where far-flung clan can meet for vacations and enjoy fun, friends, and some time on the golf course. We see it as a place where we can write in our journals, find spiritual solace, walk alone on a beach or maybe hear an uplifting symphony. Owning a vacation-to-retirement home allows us to tap into visions of a worry-free life of water activities (or mountain activities, or golf activities) – life filled with joy and leisure.

THE INVESTMENT OPPORTUNITY

A (potential) rustic mountain retreat or contemporary golf villa can be an investment with significant appreciation potential. That simple little cabin along the bay can be one of the best ways to build wealth while providing life-long fun for you and your family. After all, investing in real estate historically has been one of the best ways to develop capital.

During the past decade, second home ownership has jumped significantly, largely because of low interest rates on mortgages and the rapid appreciation of real estate prices. Motivated by those same factors along with the desire to retire in multiple locations, more people are picking up third homes too. Researchers believe that the demand for second homes is about to burgeon, as forty million baby boomers reach prime second-home-buying age.

Vacation homes offer a range of investment opportunities. Our mountains, lakes, oceans, and rivers are limited resources, so property on or near these recreational areas is likely to gain in value. As the numbers of high-income, high-asset, middle-age or older couples, who have children nearing adulthood or have no children living at home, decide to purchase that vacation-to-retirement home, that cute coastal town or that charming mountain community will be even more desirable.

Courtesy of D. Peter Lund.

Right:
Courtesy of D. Peter Lund.

Courtesy of D. Peter Lund.

Courtesy of D. Peter Lund.

Courtesy of D. Peter Lund.

Courtesy of D. Peter Lund.

Courtesy of D. Peter Lund.

THE DESIRED LIFETYLE

A vacation-to-retirement home can be a cabin or a palace, a condo, or a mobile home. To find the right one, we need to define who we are while on vacation and the type of lifestyle we desire during that time – and once we are retired.

Perhaps we are the avid fisherman who wants to live and breathe for that fish or maybe we prefer visiting the local museums and listening to the symphony. Or maybe we just want the sound of the wind on the mountaintop and a roaring fire.

In contemplating the purchase or construction of a vacation-to-retirement home, you need to analyze your primary reasons for undertaking this step.

• What is your ideal travel distance? Is a four-hour drive too long for a weekend? Distance is also an important consideration if you are planning on hosting friends and family. People are not always willing to travel long distances – especially for a brief weekend. If you will only have time to visit your new home a few weeks a year before you retire, a timeshare or rental may be more cost-effective and easier to maintain.

Designed and built in 1919 by William Hooker Gillette, a well-known actor (the original Sherlock Holmes), this castle overlooks the Connecticut River. *Courtesy of D. Peter Lund.*

• If you are just buying a vacation home, ask yourself what are your most enjoyable vacation experiences? What activities do you enjoy the most? Are those activities available in the area you are considering?

• If you are considering ultimately retiring there, you probably should consider what your needs may be as you mature. For example, you may not care now, but ultimately you may want your master bedroom on the main floor. Older knees don't always like that climb up the stairs!

18

• The question you also need to ask is what will happen if you should become incapacitated later on. If you are considering a vacation-to-retirement home, you should consider whether the house provides easy living for all ages and abilities: one-story living, wide halls, baths, and doorways, and no-step entries can make life simpler when your needs change.

• If you are considering making this your permanent residence, check it out thoroughly. Talk to other property owners; investigate municipal and property taxes, access to health care and home/auto services, noise and parking problems during the tourist season, and the availability of recreational/cultural facilities, restaurants, and shopping.

• Experts suggest renting before buying in an unfamiliar area to help determine if this is the place for you. One couple moved to Boston for three months to check it out as a possible vacation-to-retirement spot. They wanted to determine for themselves whether it was as vibrant a community as the ads said.

• What do you want in the way of services? Many people buy condos or homes in an association because they won't have to worry about maintenance. Others prefer taking care of their own necessities, doing their own work.

• Can you handle the tax implications and financing? Mortgage interest and property taxes on a second home may be tax deductible (depending upon the use you make of it), just as are the interest payments on the mortgage for your primary home. Tax laws are complicated and constantly change. Be sure to consult your professional tax advisor.

• There are also those hidden costs such as homeowner's insurance, taxes, maintenance costs, security to protect the home while you're gone, and travel expenses. And just like your primary residence, you'll pay for services such as sewer, water, electricity/gas, and phone. You may also need to consider unusual costs, such as winterizing a cabin in the mountains or adding an alarm system.

When well planned, a vacation home can offer a break from the stresses of everyday life, giving us an opportunity to recharge, relax, and gain perspective. A vacation-to-retirement home can provide us with a permanent place to spend alone or with family and friends – a time to pay attention to all the people and interests that get forgotten in our dot-com worlds.

The gateway to one of many Newport cottages. *Courtesy of D. Peter Lund.*

A Cape Cod cottage that is being renovated. *Courtesy of D. Peter Lund.*

CREATING YOUR OWN SPECIAL PLACE

Paging through this book, you will realize that finding a talented designer is the next step in the process of creating a home. Architects, builders, and designers assist people in making dreams come true – whether it is reveling in a peaceful vacation in a lakeside cabin, skiing out the door of your mountain condo, or enjoying your retirement in a new area.

There is no "right" style for a vacation-to-retirement home. The best style is that which suits the client.

BUILDING A CASTLE

A narrow peninsula of glacial origin, this three hundred ninety-nine square mile piece of Southeast Massachusetts extends sixty-five miles into the Atlantic Ocean. The Cape contains long sandy beaches, sand dunes, marshes, freshwater ponds, low hills, and historic sites.

In his book *Cape Cod,* Henry Thoreau said, "A man may stand there and put all America behind him," referring to the Outer Cape's Atlantic beach, an unbroken stretch of some thirty miles.

Cape Cod has always been linked to the sea. Many, including the Pilgrims, have looked to it to fulfill their needs and ambitions.

In 1602, an English explorer, Bartholomew Gosnold named the Cape for the abundant quantities of cod his crew managed to catch in its waters. Until the late 1800s, fishing, whaling, shipping, and salt making were important industries. In the mid-nineteenth century, the Cape saw its most prosperous days, thanks largely to the whaling industry.

During the late nineteenth century, the decline in whaling hit the Cape hard, and it began cultivating the tourist industry. In 1848, the first train service from Boston began. By 1873, it had been extended from Sandwich to Provincetown. Vacationing families came to enjoy the fresh Atlantic waters, and Cape Cod began to court visitors actively.

Tourism and cranberry growing (Cape Cod is one of the nation's major producers) are now economic mainstays. Memorial Day through Columbus Day means crowded roads, idyllic beach days, and high prices.

The Cape also offers a wonderful place for retirement. The winter and summer temperatures are milder on the Cape than on the mainland. The moderating ocean breezes, its arresting natural beauty, and the easy way of life attract many. On the other hand, housing development and population (now about 200,000) have gradu-

The clear and gentle waters of Nantucket and Vineyard Sound and Buzzards Bay caress the Cape Cod Shores. *Courtesy of D. Peter Lund.*

Notice the low windows and doors. *Courtesy of D. Peter Lund.*

ally increased, and the Cape is faced with strains on water and road systems as well as with increasing pollution.

The owners of the home under construction have known the Cape for over forty years. Her family spent summers in a charming old hunter's cabin. When she was a young girl, she and her sister would walk their Irish setter down the private lane to a nearby lake. She knows the area well.

As an owner here, she will have deeded rights to the path, the beach on the lake, as well as rights to three salt-water boat landings on the bay where she first learned to sail.

She wanted a one-level house, which meant that the lot had to be at least one hundred fifty feet wide. Like many areas, this town tries to regulate builders, which adds to the cost and increases the construction time.

The owners had a few, very specific needs. They wanted large rooms, high ceilings, and enough space for their combined family of five children. They wanted no maintenance and, therefore, will have no grass. Instead of a back lawn, they have a large curving deck with a curved metal railing. In time, they will have a Thermo Spa on the deck.

The kitchen has all the latest appliances, along with a six-burner gas range set in a curved Corian countertop. The gas fireplaces were so new that she ordered them without knowing what they would look like. She plans to mount a high definition flat television screen over the fireplace in the den. They will have a security system in the house and special lighting outside. The heat and air conditioning is hydro/air.

Courtesy of D. Peter Lund.

Here, you can see the lever door handles on this new vacation-to-retirement home.
Courtesy of D. Peter Lund.

Universal Design

In planning for a vacation-to-retirement home, we need to create a design to make our home more flexible and user-friendly for everyone.

Some call it lifestyle design. Others call it easy living. The scientific term is universal design, which means designing for the world the way it really is – with accessibility for everyone, regardless of diverse needs.

Some of the better known universal design features are:

• No-step entries, which allow everyone to enter the house.
• One-story living.
• Wider hallways (36" - 42") and doorways (32" - 36") which let wheelchairs pass through.
• More floor space, which provides greater turning radius for people in wheelchairs.
• Flush floor thresholds, which make it easy for a wheelchair and help to keep people from tripping.
• Light controls, electrical outlets, and thermostats that can be easily reached from a wheelchair.
• Lever door handles, which are great for people with poor hand strength and when your arms are full of packages.

Other universal design features that are being used in some new home construction primarily in developments marketed to people over fifty years of age include:

• Master bedroom suite on the main level.
• Readily opened windows with lower sills.
• Lower kitchen cabinets with rollout and pull-down shelving.
• Multi-level counters in the kitchen.
• Extra lighting, especially in bedrooms and bathrooms.
• Non-slip floors.
• Laundry chutes.
• No-threshold, large showers with either built-in steps or stools and grab bars.
• Raised toilets.
• Front-loading washer and dryers.

—Source: National Association of Homebuilders

Caring for your Vacation Home

Pipes burst, roofs leak, washing machines break.

Taking care of a home can be a challenge, especially when work needs to be done. It can be even harder if it is your second home.

You might visit your vacation home only several times a year. Essential services, such as gutter cleaning, pest control, lawn and pool care, and routine maintance still need to be done. You may also have to worry about the freezing winter temperatures, the occasional hurricane, or possible vandalism.

You can set up regularly scheduled maintenance programs with local contractors. Ensuring that you have dependable service providers to care for your investment or vacation property is money well spent unless you have the time or desire to do it yourself.

Because it will probably be used less than your primary home, your vacation home can have unseen problems that may escalate.

One homeowner had a caring neighbor who called to tell him that a huge ice pile was forming outside his basement window after several zero-degree days. The pipes had burst. Another had a squirrel that found his attic to be a nice new nest.

Vacation homes that are well cared for tend to maintain their value and require fewer large repairs, keeping costs down in the long run. Failing to maintain the premises of your investment property can be costly as well. When considering a purchase, you'll need to budget for maintenance costs as necessary.

Many second homeowners are eager to farm out their home repair and improvement projects but locating and hiring a good contractor can be a difficult process.

Some homeowners talk about spending months haggling with the local contractors (who may be scarce in some vacation areas) and getting little work done until they come on site. One hired a charming young man who promised to construct the new family room during the winter to find that he spent most of his time partying with his friends and fending off the local authorities.

Independent contractors and qualified handymen are available, if you search. Just as in your primary home, you will need them in your second home.

Special care needs to be taken to guard against unwanted and potentially dangerous home invasions when the property is unoccupied.

A burglar is a non-professional criminal who looks at the crime as an opportunity to take advantage of a situation. Generally, they slip in and out of a house, taking only what is readily accessible.

Studies show that a burglar will go elsewhere if it takes more than four or five minutes to break into a home.

Make it difficult and maybe a burglar won't come to your house.

Make your home appear "lived-in"

Invest in a good programmable timer. It can be programmed so that it varies the way it lights the home at night. Try to give the impression that your house is occupied when you are away.

Ask a friend or your caretaker to occasionally park a car in your driveway.

Insure that all doors and windows are locked when the home is not occupied. Over 60% of residential burglaries happen during the day. Failing to secure all doors and windows when leaving home, even for a few minutes, is one of the most common mistakes leading to home robberies. A local neighborhood child can turn into a burglar if all he/she has to do is walk through an unlocked door or crawl through an open window.

If you are out back, don't leave the front door open. Anyone can walk in and happily steal the family silver. That happened to our family friends one warm summer day. She was ready to set the table and had left the room to answer the phone. Some lucky thief walked through the French doors and absconded with the entire silver chest.

All exterior doors should be metal clad or solid hardwood because they cannot be easily battered down or forced open.

If you have sliding glass doors, place a length of wood in the lower track. Make sure it fits snugly and cannot be popped out of the track by an intruder. You can also talk to your locksmith about a Charley bar, which attaches to the side frame and folds down across the glass, bracing itself against the opposite frame.

Obviously, don't leave a note on your door telling people that you are not at home! That note could become an invitation.

Get an alarm – and use it!

Yes, they are a nuisance and expensive, but they certainly help. My friend wrote that while they were gone, a burglar tried to get in their house, but the alarm frightened him off. Invest in a good alarm. And if you already have one, use it. How many people have one and never put it on?

Since many vacation homes are in more rural areas, you may also want to get an alarm that monitors your home temperature. Alarms can alert you to changes in temperature, water leakage, and power outages in your home, computer room, or greenhouse. They also give you the power to turn your heat on from anywhere, using a touchtone phone (with the installation of a second thermostat).

Consider a dog (stuffed will do)

My friend bought a large stuffed black dog, which is peering out from behind a corner in the kitchen. He looks big, bold, and mean! A burglar would definitely think twice. To further this image, leave out a dog bowl and leash.

Get a safe

A safe is a good place to put those important papers, passports, and jewelry.

Don't live in a fishbowl

Don't leave expensive items in direct view of open windows. Keep your shades and drapes drawn at night. A lighted house with open drapes exposes its contents to every passerby.

Trim shrubs so windows and doors are in full view from the street. Unobstructed doors and windows are a deterrent because the intruder is forced to work in the open where detection is likely. Have adequate lighting, especially at vulnerable entry points.

Never discuss the contents of your home with anyone outside of your family. Most of us love to talk about our belongings or show them off. But we could be asking for major trouble.

Consider those garage doors

Never leave your garage door opener in an unlocked car. To do so could give burglars access to your garage. If you have an attached garage, you could also be giving them entry to your home! If you keep your garage doors locked, you can prevent burglars from entering your home through the door leading from the attached garage to the house.

Find a trusted friend

Ask him or her to pick up your mail (unless you have the post office hold it until your return) and gather up newspapers, litter, packages, or anything else that could alert a burglar to the fact that your home is unoccupied. If possible, have someone park in your driveway or in front of your home, mow the lawn or shovel sidewalks, and bring in your trash cans.

Meet your neighbors

Get to know your neighbors, and report any suspicious characters to your local police department immediately.

Watch the telephone

Program an answering machine. Change the message occasionally and check the messages often. If you are a woman living alone and you have a listed telephone number, have the number listed under your initials or under a male relative's name. Do not use your first name in the listing, and NEVER include your address in the listing. Even better, have a male friend or relative's voice on your answering machine.

Never reveal personal information

Telephone solicitors and strangers may have other motives. If you answer their questions, they can learn about your habits and discover the contents of your home. There is no need to respond to an unknown caller's questions.

Never open your door to a stranger

Instruct your children to do the same. Keep your door closed and locked unless you know who is on the other side of it. You can install a 180-degree wide-angle viewer to see who is at the door before opening it. These viewers are available from locksmiths and hardware stores.

Protect your keys

Remove all keys hidden around the property. Don't have your name and/or address imprinted on a key tag or your license. If you must leave a key with a parking attendant, leave the key to the car's ignition only. Take all other keys with you.

Planning

The best way to minimize your risk is through careful and proactive planning. You need to ensure that your home is safe from fire and other potential hazards. You need to eradicate the clutter and inspect your home for possible hazards. Before you leave after the season, you need to inspect your home thoroughly.

An insurance professional well versed in vacation and investment properties is essential. When insuring a second home, you need to have the right coverage for liability, replacement and/or repair, and natural disasters. Make sure your coverage protects every aspect of your property including outbuildings and structures such as guest cottages, storage sheds, boathouses, or docks.

Courtesy of D. Peter Lund.

GRAND AND GLORIOUS HOMES

"Where are our castles now, where are our towers"? lamented Sir Thomas More (1478-1535). Today, we can find them in many beautiful places – from mountaintops to cities, from sparkling waterfront to verdant valleys.

Courtesy of D. Peter Lund.

Courtesy of D. Peter Lund.

MOUNTAINTOP RESIDENCE

Inspired by the Anasazi sculptural stone and plaster villages, Sears Barrett AIA, carved this residence into a mountaintop above Evergreen, Colorado. The steel-framed structure is built on a plan of interlocking, elongated hexagons.

The central space of this home is a true great room, with the living room, informal dining room, kitchen, and a study alcove all gathered in one sunlit space.

A forty foot indoor swimming pool provides a unique opportunity to swim while enjoying views of snow-covered mountaintops.

Floor-to-ceiling, insulated curved glass panels dissolve the feeling of corners. Interior passages and stairs are formed in a similar fashion, creating the sense of a home molded out of stone and plaster.

Curved horizontal roof and deck planes with deep cantilevers convey the impression of the structure floating above the stone piers. *Courtesy of Sears Barrett.*

Tapered stone piers supporting roof planes of sculptural stucco are the basic components inspired by Anasazi cliff dwellings. *Courtesy of Sears Barrett.*

26

Large expanses of glass, curving walls of stone or plaster, and heated slate floors are the basic set of materials used throughout. *Courtesy of Tim Murphy.*

The formal zone of the house is another grand space that unifies the dining room, living room, and entry stair. *Courtesy of Tim Murphy.*

Flanking the great room fireplace are French doors that open to the swimming pool. The pool can also be accessed via a circular stair to the children's playroom below. The 40' pool is shaped in an elongated hexagon that mirrors the basic design module of the house. Heated sandstone floors and rubble stone walls provide a strong mountain ambience. *Courtesy of Tim Murphy.*

A smooth maple ceiling plays off the rich texture of the rubble stonewall in the master bedroom. The floor-to-ceiling glass opens the view to foothills in the day and city lights below at night. *Courtesy of Tim Murphy.*

ARTS & CRAFTS COTTAGE

Trained as an engineer, this homeowner was fascinated by the relationship of art and technology. He decided to devote each of his homes to a different period and/or theme; a wooded beachfront lot on Lake Michigan became home to his Arts & Crafts, Mission, and Southwest collections as well as a retreat for his extended family

Architect Sandy Vitzthum's mission was to design a predominantly English Arts & Crafts cottage that was to reflect the all the crafts movements at the turn of the century. The result is a cottage with symmetrical rigor that is softened by rich materials: cedar, brick, oak, woven fabrics, hammered silver, stained glass, and, of course, field flowers.

Because the client entertained often, the cottage also had to work as well for a bachelor as for a house party of twenty-four, or even a party for one hundred.

The house is approached formally, with a simple basin to mark the axis of the avenue and the house's center. The house's shape is simple with the typical English triple gable. The upper floors' shingling is more refined than the ground floor. Vitzthun rusticated the lower level by doubling up the shingles for heavier shadow lines. She also widened the exposure. ©2002 Carolyn L. Bates – carolynbates.com.

The Michigan woods are omnipresent. ©2002 Carolyn L. Bates – carolynbates.com

The view from the lake. ©2002 Carolyn L. Bates – carolynbates.com.

Climbing roses are the only adornment for the entry. The custom mahogany front door has hand-forged straps and an antique knocker. ©2002 Carolyn L. Bates – carolynbates.com.

The rough-hewn porch receives full morning and afternoon sun. ©2002 Carolyn L. Bates – carolynbates.com.

A turn-of-the-century house in Massachusetts inspired the diamond shingle skirt. ©2002 Carolyn L. Bates – carolynbates.com.

The top of the chimney is noteworthy; it features a "birdhouse." ©2002 Carolyn L. Bates – carolynbates.com.

The primary rooms are on the second floor (piano nobile) of the house, so the entry hall simply prepares one to climb up. The stairs, a replica of those at William Morris' Red House, are made from rift-cut quarter sawn white oak. ©2002 Carolyn L. Bates – carolynbates.com.

Lutyens inspired the vaulted fireplace. Batchelder Studio (c. 1910) made the 12" tile. ©2002 Carolyn L. Bates – carolynbates.com.

A family room with a heavy, vaulted fireplace along with two garages are on the ground floor. ©2002 Carolyn L. Bates – carolynbates.com.

Books and artifacts line the walls. Extra spaces are filled with stained-glass study drawings and terra cotta fragments. ©2002 Carolyn L. Bates – carolynbates.com.

The library is lofty and bright. The oak colonettes to the high ceiling living room can be seen above the stairs. ©2002 Carolyn L. Bates – carolynbates.com.

The three main bedrooms are at the ends of the house; the master bedroom is Gothic with William Morris' "Compton" upholstery and rug. Vitzthun designed the Gothic four-poster bed from rift-cut quarter sawn oak. ©2002 Carolyn L. Bates – carolynbates.com.

The doors are the flat-paneled "Christian Cross" type popular at the turn of the century. The hinges have steeple tips; thumb latches were used rather than handles. *©2002 Carolyn L. Bates – carolynbates.com.*

The living room has a massive Indiana limestone fireplace and an oak balcony that carries the theme of the stairs through the house. Both the living and dining room have an abundance of Morris fabrics, and the living room rug is an authentic Morris design. *©2002 Carolyn L. Bates – carolynbates.com.*

This bedroom is homage to the Mission style, with a collection of southwestern etchings. ©2002 Carolyn L. Bates – carolynbates.com.

This room is bright with Morris' "Honeysuckle" wallpaper, an authentic Voysey-designed rug of stylized honeysuckle, family heirloom beds, and portraits. ©2002 Carolyn L. Bates – carolynbates.com.

The bunk suite contains two rooms, each sleeping seven people, and a bath. The dorm style bath allows several people to use it at once. ©2002 Carolyn L. Bates – carolynbates.com.

Below the screened porch is the tub porch.
©2002 Carolyn L. Bates –
carolynbates.com.

The screened porch off of
the dining room has
exposed cedar and pine
walls and ceiling. ©2002
Carolyn L. Bates –
carolynbates.com.

SALT AIR AND SEASPRAY

City dwellers have enjoyed second homes in the country since the post Civil War economic boom. Barefooted and bathing suited, they have thrived in "the simple summer life" in age-old oceanfront villages.

Today, many of these summer cottages have been replaced by year-around vacation homes, which have all the comforts of suburbia. With increased population and increased desire for vacation and/or retirement homes, open land has dwindled.

The designation of the Cape Cod National Seashore in 1966 spared nearly 43,557 acres of Atlantic Ocean coastline from development. It includes forty miles of pristine sandy beach, salt marshes, swamps, groves of pine, maple, oak, and cedar, and dozens of sparkling saltwater and clear, freshwater kettle ponds. A variety of historic structures throughout the area capture the charm of the New England coast.

Immersed in the sea air, this one-time summer house overlooking the seashore has remained in the family for several generations. Today, it has become a full-time residence rich with history and memories.

Rather than becoming a seaside retrofit, this house has retained its memories and its old woodwork. *Courtesy of D. Peter Lund.*

Several generations of family and friends have enjoyed dinners in this room. *Courtesy of D. Peter Lund.*

The owner is a gifted artist. *Courtesy of D. Peter Lund.*

The lone bird watches over all.
Courtesy of D. Peter Lund.

Childhood treasures from one generation remain
for the next. *Courtesy of D. Peter Lund.*

You can see the endlessly rolling waves from these windows. *Courtesy of D. Peter Lund.*

The bathrooms are from a more gentle age. *Courtesy of D. Peter Lund.*

Let the sun shine in! *Courtesy of D. Peter Lund.*

The kitchen reminds us of grandmothers, aprons, and homemade chocolate chip cookies. *Courtesy of D. Peter Lund.*

The bedrooms haven't changed much over the years. The sheets are probably drip dry rather than cotton, but the quilts are still colorful and warm on those cold June nights. *Courtesy of D. Peter Lund.*

Life is good. You can swim, play tennis, sail, fish, or just watch the endless variations of the ocean. *Courtesy of D. Peter Lund.*

The grounds of this family estate lend themselves to weddings, family celebrations, and long walks. *Courtesy of D. Peter Lund.*

Imagine a bride walking down this aisle.
Courtesy of D. Peter Lund.

The flag flies everyday.
Courtesy of D. Peter Lund.

Beauty is around every corner. *Courtesy of D. Peter Lund.*

Everywhere you look another oasis of peace awaits.
Courtesy of D. Peter Lund.

Just stretch your legs and bask out in the sun.
Courtesy of D. Peter Lund.

Even the cutting garden has its
adornment. *Courtesy of D. Peter Lund.*

THE GUEST HOUSES

The Cape is endlessly appealing. The crashing ocean beaches, gentle bay beaches with their dazzling sunsets, and tranquil freshwater ponds draw visitors here. They come for the fun of the beach towns, the beauty of the white sand, that lovely ocean breeze – and your beautiful home. The Guest Houses are part of the estate pictured on page 42.

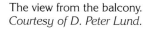

The view from the balcony.
Courtesy of D. Peter Lund.

The best of all possible worlds is when guests can stay in your guesthouse. This estate has several. *Courtesy of D. Peter Lund.*

The second guesthouse.
Courtesy of D. Peter Lund.

The large family room in one guesthouse.
Courtesy of D. Peter Lund.

One of the many beds and baths that await the fortunate guest. *Courtesy of D. Peter Lund.*

Playing in Paradise

Luxury co-ops and condominiums, townhouses, and pieds-a-terre: some elect to live in the city for their vacation and retirement. They want to participate in that metro energy.

Waterford Waterfront Properties, Inc. is developing luxurious waterfront condominiums overlooking the Intracoastal Waterway on Venice Island in Florida. These architecturally stunning residences tower above an enclave of boutiques, restaurants, theaters, tennis courts, the water, and the bridge.

A gated security entry and covered parking help to make living easy. *Courtesy of D. Peter Lund.*

The 18' x 15' living room has great views of the water. The 18' x 8' foot terrace has even better views and fresh breezes! *Courtesy of D. Peter Lund.*

A small wet bar adds elegance. *Courtesy of D. Peter Lund.*

The elegant maintenance-free living includes a cabana, heated pool, fitness center, and boat docks. *Courtesy of D. Peter Lund.*

The washer and dryer are closeted away.
Courtesy of D. Peter Lund.

The library permits escape. *Courtesy of D. Peter Lund.*

Granite kitchen countertops with raised panel custom wood cabinets add to the elegance of the kitchen. *Courtesy of D. Peter Lund.*

The master bedroom provides for that private viewing of city lights reflected in the waterway at night and the drawbridge lights.
Courtesy of D. Peter Lund.

Of course, living here gives you community boat docks and concierge boat storage located near several marinas.
Courtesy of D. Peter Lund.

The luxurious master bath contains all the possible amenities including a walk-in Roman shower and garden tub. *Courtesy of D. Peter Lund.*

HIDDEN LAKE LODGE

This home by Alan Mascord Design Associates won several awards, including the People's Choice Best of Show and the Realtor's Choice Best Curb Appeal at the 2004 Portland Street of Dreams.

An artful use of stone was employed on the exterior of this rustic hillside home. This use of stone complements other architectural elements such as the angled, oversize four-car garage and the substantial roofline. *Courtesy of Bob Greenspan.*

The entrance is welcoming. *Courtesy of Bob Greenspan.*

The floor plan features an enormous great room as its hub, anchored with a large stone fireplace at one end. *Courtesy of Bob Greenspan.*

The well-appointed kitchen has easy-to-reach appliances. *Courtesy of Bob Greenspan.*

The kitchen has a walk-in pantry and snack-bar counter. *Courtesy of Bob Greenspan.*

The great room has a massive vaulted ceiling. *Courtesy of Bob Greenspan.*

A formal dining area anchors one end of the great room. *Courtesy of Bob Greenspan.*

At the other end of the great room is the home office. *Courtesy of Bob Greenspan.*

The kitchen opens on to a large porch. *Courtesy of Bob Greenspan.*

Its appointments include a cook top and a corner fireplace. *Courtesy of Bob Greenspan.*

The master suite is found at the other side of the home. As with all of the Alan Mascord Design Associates homes shown here, this house offers one-story living for the homeowner. Eating, bathing, and sleeping are all located on one, barrier-free level. *Courtesy of Bob Greenspan.*

There are expansive his and hers walk-in closets, a spa tub, a skylit double vanity area, and a corner fireplace in the salon. *Courtesy of Bob Greenspan.*

Three family bedrooms are on the lower level. *Courtesy of Bob Greenspan.*

55

There is a wine cellar and a wet bar. *Courtesy of Bob Greenspan.*

The bathrooms are luxuriously appointed throughout. *Courtesy of Bob Greenspan.*

The home theater has a built-in viewing screen, a fireplace, and double terrace access. *Courtesy of Bob Greenspan.*

It also has trains! *Courtesy of Bob Greenspan.*

This grand house even has a dog shower and grooming station just off the garage. *Courtesy of Bob Greenspan.*

Vacation-to-Retirement Compound

In the 1970s, a childless couple built this house from a generic kit designed and built by a local home center. They located it on a home site across a tidal marsh from the harbor side beach. The Atlantic Ocean lies just beyond the barrier beach located across the harbor.

Unfortunately, when built, the original house plans were not customized to maximize the benefits of the waterfront site.

In 1997, the present owners purchased the home for a long-term vacation home. They asked Mark Farber Architect to undertake a whole house remodeling and renovation.

The new owners wanted a house that would better suit their desires for an active outdoor lifestyle for their extended family, their guests, and neighbors. Today, during the summer months and holidays, it serves a family of six, including parents, three young daughters, a grandmother, five dogs, and numerous guests.

The addition of smaller scaled elements like porches, pergolas, bays, and dormers serve to give the bland original structure a more intimate character.

The majority of the house additions were in outdoor living areas, which expanded the house in all directions. Farber enlarged the house by creating a "compound" of small outbuildings adjacent to the main house. To unify these structures, each outbuilding has exterior painted trim and cedar wall and roof shingles, similar to the main house. As a result, the house was expanded in all directions.

The main house "remodeling" had only a series of small additions made to it at appropriate areas to make each existing room more functional and better sited to its location. Farber designed cross ventilation into every room to promote natural cooling from the sea breezes. *Courtesy of D. Peter Lund.*

On the brick foundation of an old water well pit and gazebo, a new guest house was built with recycled fir beams. *Courtesy of D. Peter Lund.*

The interior was finished with Port Orford cedar. *Courtesy of D. Peter Lund.*

A sleeping loft is reached by a ship's ladder.
Courtesy of D. Peter Lund.

A collapsing shed was re-built with rough-sawn pine posts, beams, and sheathing to become a home office for the husband, an avid fisherman. A white, rose-covered picket fence and arbor link the fishing shed to the house. *Courtesy of D. Peter Lund.*

A fish-cleaning station makes cleaning fish a breeze and keeps that messy task out of the main kitchen. *Courtesy of D. Peter Lund.*

The shed serves to store all fishing gear. *Courtesy of D. Peter Lund.*

An existing garden shed was converted to store boating and beach equipment. *Courtesy of D. Peter Lund.*

A gravel driveway, with granite cobblestone edging, unifies the random siting of the buildings. *Courtesy of D. Peter Lund.*

The original narrow galley kitchen/laundry/hall was doubled in size toward the backyard to incorporate eating area, bar area, desk area, and a window seat. *Courtesy of D. Peter Lund.*

Brick and stone patios were added on all sides of the house to promote outdoor living. New doorways open the house to these new outdoor living areas. A front porch was added to provide shelter from the rain and a place to drink coffee as the sun rises over the ocean. A pergola, deck, and brick patio were built to allow the formally isolated living room to take advantage of the southern exposure and views of the harbor and ocean beyond. *Courtesy of D. Peter Lund.*

French casement windows open the kitchen to
views and sea breezes. *Courtesy of D. Peter Lund.*

In his work, Farber
designed a system
of recycled Heart
Pine posts and beams
to transfer the existing
roof loads to the new
outer walls, while
organizing the large,
low-ceilinged,
open space for multiple
uses. *Courtesy of D.
Peter Lund.*

The bar area includes its own refrigerator and icemaker, making preparation easy for trips on the boat or to the beach. The laundry was relocated into a portion of the existing over-sized, two-car garage. *Courtesy of D. Peter Lund.*

Details. *Courtesy of D. Peter Lund.*

Life goes on in this kitchen.
Courtesy of D. Peter Lund.

The previously glass-enclosed, dark-stained wood "Florida Room" was totally renovated with all new walls, window, interior finishes, and heating added to allow for full-year living. A large, three-sided bay, with arched ceiling, expands the room and provides panoramic views of the salt pond, marsh, harbor, and ocean beyond. It's the perfect place to do jigsaw puzzles on rainy days. The brick fireplace takes the chill off New England summer evenings and warms the room on even the coldest winter nights. *Courtesy of D. Peter Lund.*

A wainscot of beaded wood encircling the room provides a cottage-feel to the room. Built-in shelves display books and the owner's working decoy collection. Recycled Heart Pine beams give the room a sense of age, while linking the room to the adjacent kitchen, which was built with the same materials. *Courtesy of D. Peter Lund.*

With views of the harbor, fish piers, and lighthouse beyond, the living room provides a quiet retreat from the rest of the house. Flanking the large windows, French doors provide access to the pergola, deck, and semi-circular brick patio. *Courtesy of D. Peter Lund.*

Space was "borrowed" from the attic to raise the ceiling of the master bedroom two and one-half feet higher than its original seven foot ceiling height. *Courtesy of D. Peter Lund.*

The existing truss-framed roof was re-engineered, and the remaining structural trusses were left exposed and trimmed with painted poplar wood. An assemblage of windows creates a backdrop for the bed and headboard and captures dramatic views of the harbor and ocean beyond. *Courtesy of D. Peter Lund.*

This bedroom is a safe and charming haven. The simple, white-painted trim, seen here and throughout the interior and exterior, furthers the "cottage-style" look. *Courtesy of D. Peter Lund.*

A cushioned window seat fills a dormer, providing a cozy spot to watch sea birds. Dimmable sconce lights give a warm glow at night. *Courtesy of D. Peter Lund.*

Custom built-in furnishings personalize each living space. *Courtesy of D. Peter Lund.*

With the addition of a large shed dormer, bathroom, built-in dressers, and heat, the previously underutilized room above the garage became a bunkroom for the two older daughters and many sleepover guests. With its own staircase and its remote location, the bunkroom is acoustically isolated from the rest of the house. Separately zoned, this room can be closed off when the kids move out. *Courtesy of D. Peter Lund.*

A reading nook located above the back staircase provides a cozy retreat with its many pillows. *Courtesy of D. Peter Lund.*

Guests find a warm welcome here. *Courtesy of D. Peter Lund.*

They can just stretch out and
reflect on the way of the world.
Courtesy of D. Peter Lund.

Many architectural details adorn the house. Circular
windows promote a nautical theme, which is furthered by
onion lamps. The use of recycled exposed posts and beams
provide a sense of age to the house, while the wide knotty
pine flooring gives an informal quality to the house. An
arched footbridge and raised wooden boardwalk were built
to provide access across the marsh to the harbor side
beach, shellfish-laden flats, and moored boats beyond.
Courtesy of D. Peter Lund.

HILLSIDE DESIGN

Hillside designs offer the best solutions to sites that have slopes. Alan Mascord Design Associates' Craftsman is not only spacious and accommodating but a visual treat.

The angled main entry is impressive. *Courtesy of Dan Tyrpak.*

It opens to a main level that is rife with livability.
Courtesy of Dan Tyrpak

The gracious entry foyer.
Courtesy of Bob Greenspan.

It contains a grand staircase with double entry to the lower level. *Courtesy of Bob Greenspan.*

This is a wonderful room to listen to some Bach or maybe some jazz. *Courtesy of Bob Greenspan.*

Doorways are wide, which would allow a wheelchair if necessary. *Courtesy of Bob Greenspan.*

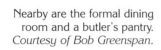

Nearby are the formal dining room and a butler's pantry. *Courtesy of Bob Greenspan.*

The island kitchen provides ample work space. *Courtesy of Bob Greenspan.*

It includes all the latest equipment. *Courtesy of Bob Greenspan.*

A nook with patio access complements the space. *Courtesy of Bob Greenspan.*

The master suite is fit for a prince or a princess. *Courtesy of Bob Greenspan.*

The den is accessed from the left side of the foyer. *Courtesy of Bob Greenspan.*

The bath is exceptionally well appointed. A laundry and half-bath complete the main level. *Courtesy of Bob Greenspan.*

A games room on the lower level has a fireplace and media center, plus double doors to a covered patio. The lower level also offers three additional bedrooms – each with a private bath. *Courtesy of Bob Greenspan.*

There is also a wine cellar, a computer center, a wet bar, a home theater, and a laundry room. *Courtesy of Bob Greenspan.*

ARTS & CRAFTS STYLE VACATION HOUSE

Carmel by the Sea in California combines the charm of a small town with stunning natural beauty. The town is nestled in an urban forest and surrounded by the crashing surf of the Pacific Ocean. This architecturally dramatic, newly constructed vacation home is located just off the beach amidst the beautiful oak and pine trees.

The client hired Debra Kay George Interiors after the house was purchased but before construction began. Ms. George made some alterations to the original floor plan, customizing it to accommodate the needs and lifestyles of the owners. She worked with the client to create a home of rustic beauty with a truly inviting and relaxing atmosphere.

The site is sprinkled with existing pine, cypress, and oak trees. The home weaves its away around these trees and fits into them like an old rambling cabin in the woods. *Courtesy of John Canham.*

Opposite page, bottom left:
The dining room is semi formal. Artist Jon Hunt painted a mural of the local historic Carmel mission on the large wall. This mural adds interest and uniqueness to the room. *Courtesy of John Canham.*

Opposite page, bottom right:
The blue, green, gold, and terra cotta tones of the mural are repeated in the fabrics and rug. The rug is a Stickley in the Arts & Crafts style, which creates a welcome blend with the Country French table and hutch. *Courtesy of John Canham.*

The home was built by Robert W. Hayes & Associates, Architects and Planners, and designed in the Arts & Crafts or Craftsman style. Craftsman elements include wire-brushed cedar beams and cabinets, oil-rubbed bronze hinges and hardware, art glass light fixtures, wrought iron, oak floors, and stone. *Courtesy of John Canham.*

To the left of the front door is the living room where Carmel stone (from the original residence on the lot) is used on the striking fireplace. Rustic leather furnishings, distressed wood, and warm neutral tones enhance the Arts & Crafts style. These features, along with the leaf motif on the wool area rug and textured grass window shades, complement the home's natural surroundings. The armoire houses a TV and stereo components but closes up from view when not in use. *Courtesy of John Canham.*

The kitchen and breakfast nook are adjacent to the dining room. Natural limestone covers the floor, and the counters are black granite. The Craftsman style cabinets and ceiling are wire-brushed cedar. These, along with sophisticated appliances, architectural lighting, and Carmel stone, give the kitchen a warm feel. The stove adds to the ambiance. *Courtesy of John Canham.*

The breakfast nook has a lovely view of the courtyard. Floral fabrics, lighter wood tones, and whimsical art create a room with a fun, casual feeling. The custom tables and chairs have hand-painted leaves and a rubbed back finish. *Courtesy of John Canham.*

A cozy guest bedroom, office, and bathroom are at the top of one stairwell. The bedroom is furnished with an antique iron bed and custom bedding in a blue French Provencal color scheme. *Courtesy of John Canham.*

The master suite is reached through a second set of stairs at the other end of the home. To provide interest, beams, which tie into the look of the real ceiling beams, were faux painted around the door. First, the wire brush texture was applied; the wood graining technique was followed by shadowing to create truly realistic beams. A true tromp l'oeil! *Courtesy of John Canham.*

Step into the master bath and be surrounded by casual luxury. Limestone flows from sink, to shower, to tub. In addition, there are stylish faucets and a wonderful view of the lower courtyard from the windows above the soaking tub. *Courtesy of John Canham.*

The courtyard is a wonderful place to relax, dine, or entertain. *Courtesy of John Canham.*

This home brings nature inside through the courtyard. Its beautiful landscaping can be viewed through many doors and windows. *Courtesy of John Canham.*

CONTEMPORARY COLORADO LIVING

Designed by Sears Barrett AIA, this residence has an air of sculptural playfulness. The roof forms of the house, which are framed in curved laminated beams and clad in standing seam copper, resemble large ocean waves. Smooth turned logs act as massive posts to support the curving ceilings. Together with the beams, they provide a clear expression of structure.

Site topography and drainage issues led to the initial concept of separate building masses connected by bridges. Beyond the site constraints, there was a desire to develop a more horizontal massing scheme, which would reduce the scale of the structure from the street above. Comprised of three forms connected by timber-framed bridges, the house does not disturb the natural flow of surface water on the sloping thirty-five acre site.

The center form includes all the living spaces together, with guest bedrooms below. A bridge joins the center pavilion to the garage spaces on the east and a two-bedroom pavilion on the west.

The interiors are designed to create the feel of a warm, contemporary loft. With walls of glass opening to the rolling foothill views and curving ribs overhead, the roof form evokes the hull of a boat. The use of slate and bamboo flooring coupled with a palette of sand and clay tones on the walls complement the sense of living in nature.

This is an honest expression of contemporary Colorado living – open, adventurous, and keyed to a magnificent forest setting.

Viewed from the southwest, one can see the layered curved roofs. The bridge connects the central pavilion to the bedroom wing and the rocky foothills landscape. *Courtesy of J. Curtis Photography.*

The interior structure of planed logs and curved beams made of glu-lams is clearly expressed and repeated on the entry side of the residence. Overlapping curved roofs suggest the play of waves and signal the architectural surprises within. *Courtesy of J. Curtis Photography.*

A stream flows under the bridge, which accentuates the sensation, when crossing the bridge, of momentarily stepping outdoors. *Courtesy of J. Curtis Photography.*

The bedroom pavilion from uphill is nestled in the trees and provides a gentle, compatible roof form with the foothills beyond. *Courtesy of J. Curtis Photography.*

The south elevation is open to a sweeping tree-top view over the foothills.
Courtesy of J. Curtis Photography.

The first interior experience of the home is standing in the entryway flanked by two turned logs with the curved beams flowing from inside to out – a theme repeated throughout the residence. *Courtesy of Ron Rusico.*

A curving staircase set under a green house connects the lower level bedrooms and playroom to the main floor. *Courtesy of Ron Rusico.*

Late afternoon sun streams into the great room, which offers views of the rolling foothills to the south. The spiral stair leads to a play loft above the kitchen. *Courtesy of Ron Rusico.*

Slate and bamboo floors, a stained plaster fireplace surround, and the glowing tones of the post and beam structure provide a warm palette of materials. *Courtesy of Ron Rusico.*

A soaring sense of space, light entering from high clerestories, and a stepping roof form lend energy to the dynamic space. *Courtesy of Ron Rusico.*

Set to the front of the house, the office provides a glimpse of the entry as well as larger view through the glass doors to the living room. *Courtesy of Ron Rusico.*

The clients are avid art collectors and requested a mix of opportunities for displaying both paintings and sculpture. Cast and stained concrete was used for the hearth and fireplace surround. *Courtesy of Ron Rusico.*

Right:
Based on gently curving forms both in plan and section, the kitchen is nestled below a play loft. *Courtesy of Ron Rusico.*

Finished in a mix of hardwood veneers and stainless steel, the kitchen opens to the family room and provides a view from the sink over the stair to the green house and bridge beyond. *Courtesy of Ron Rusico.*

The master bedroom provides an alcove for the bed with dressing and bathing areas behind the fireplace wall. *Courtesy of Ron Rusico.*

The curved glu-lams move inside to outside providing a sun-visor and covered porch off the master bedroom. *Courtesy of Ron Rusico.*

OVERLOOKING THE INTRACOASTAL WATERWAY

Gulf coast living means sparkling water, tropical breezes, and immaculately landscaped boulevards with canopies of stately trees enhancing the feeling of tranquility. It means an active lifestyle and a full range of social activities. It also can mean Northern Italian architecture and beautifully landscaped boulevards that date back to the original city plans of 1925 for Venice, Florida.

The entrance into the gated community is lined with rustling palms. *Courtesy of D. Peter Lund.*

Designed by its owner, this beautiful house lies in a community on the waterways. *Courtesy of D. Peter Lund.*

This is Florida. The house has a large extended lanai with heated spa. *Courtesy of D. Peter Lund.*

That meets everyone's requirements. *Courtesy of D. Peter Lund.*

Dining is lovely outside.
Courtesy of D. Peter Lund.

Especially when you have the right high-tech equipment. *Courtesy of D. Peter Lund.*

And the poolside wet bar.
Courtesy of D. Peter Lund.

The house combines true hands-on craftsman-ship with innovative high-tech designs. In the great room, the tray ceiling peaks to a towering skylight. *Courtesy of D. Peter Lund.*

The great room wet bar. *Courtesy of D. Peter Lund.*

The home office. *Courtesy of D. Peter Lund.*

The kitchen allows for many guests. *Courtesy of D. Peter Lund.*

The dumbwaiter to the garage makes life that much easier. *Courtesy of D. Peter Lund.*

There's a wide array of beds and baths for friends and family. *Courtesy of D. Peter Lund.*

AMBIANCE IN RETIREMENT

This ultra-contemporary hillside plan by Alan Mascord Design Associates, Inc. has some amazing details – such as a glass floor – that add style to its appearance and comfort to its livability. Extensive fenestration on the exterior takes advantage of ambient light on the inside.

This design offers a floor plan filled with amenities and special appointments. *Courtesy of Bob Greenspan.*

The upper level has a delightful entry foyer with stone columns, a bench, and a niche. *Courtesy of Bob Greenspan.*

To the right is the open stairway to the lower level with a wall of windows on one side and a glass floor on the other. *Courtesy of Bob Greenspan*.

A wet bar connects the vaulted dining room to the professional-style kitchen. *Courtesy of Bob Greenspan*.

The dining room cabinet takes advantage of the light. *Courtesy of Bob Greenspan*.

This kitchen has all the latest conveniences including the walk-in pantry.
Courtesy of Bob Greenspan.

A vaulted nook with sliding doors to a patio
is adjoining. *Courtesy of Bob Greenspan.*

Step into the vaulted great room.
Courtesy of Bob Greenspan.

The great room also opens to the patio (note the outdoor grill and fireplace).
A large laundry is close by. *Courtesy of Bob Greenspan.*

The lavatories are state of the art. *Courtesy of Bob Greenspan.*

A sumptuous bath complements the master bedroom. *Courtesy of Bob Greenspan.*

The glass ceiling and stairs. The lower-level patio area is reached from a second bedroom or the game room. *Courtesy of Bob Greenspan.*

On the lower level you'll find a game room with built-in entertainment center, three family bedrooms, another laundry area, and a snack-bar area. *Courtesy of Bob Greenspan.*

MEADOWMERE HOUSE

Set in the Southampton's historic village, this 4,500 square foot Tudor style house is nestled in two acres of pristine landscaping. "Little Disney," as it was called, is constructed of historic clinker brick and is the sister to a larger "Big Disney," which is situated nearby. Actress Eva Gabor owned the house at one time. Campion A. Platt Architect, PC, was asked to renovate it.

In the living room, Platt channeled the elegant country hunting lodge aesthetic with coffered ceilings, thick walls, marquetry in the floors, replete with animal finials, modern leather, and cow skin tables. Employing the country light from all the large French doors throughout the room, Platt drew from the palette of the surrounding landscaping, the rich greens, and climbing wisteria. The soft white/creams balanced by the cooler urban coloring provided the clean backdrop for both the owner's classic furniture and the contemporary custom furnishings.

Located one block from the beach and sitting on a natural preserve, the house evokes a powerful country elegant character of its own.

At a corner of the living room, a pear wood desk "the LaGuardia desk" was designed as a reference and feature table.

An upper level lounge room centers on a millinery weave carpet. The crystal white couches and club chairs balanced by black and grey stained beach wood and raffia paneling and mid-century black and white photography offer a quiet and private retreat away from the more public rooms.

The stairs feature a series of elliptical furnishings: a found wood curved railing, custom sisal carpet, and skin drum table inspired by a trip to Taos, New Mexico. The1800s wooden mannequin with a coat of arms lends a traditional aspect to the room amidst the otherwise thoroughly modern coloring.

The upper level of the turret was a small secret room accessible from the upper lounge. Redesigned as a game and reading room, it became the "getaway" room, replete with a full bar. Soft silk curtains and pillows surround the custom designed leather and snakeskin backgammon table.

Utilizing a long, narrow, and uninviting rear yard, a Japanese rock garden was conceived. Over a canopied eave, the meditation platform sits above riverbed rock as a stream with traditional crawling juniper groundcover for scale. An extended open trellis beyond provides a quiet outdoor breakfast room.

The enclosed terrace connected the two otherwise disparate wings of the house to form the "great room" as an exterior space. With a glassed trellis top covered in wisteria, this organizing room was made accessible to all the main rooms of the house.

CALIFORNIA DESIGN

This residence is sited on a twenty-acre agricultural parcel among orchards and alfalfa fields in California's Central Valley. The retired client surrounded himself with icons that represented his life's work: farmland and trucks. He wanted a house that would be striking but straightforward. Avila Design designed the residence for a self-made, yet self-effacing man who wished to celebrate his accomplishments in a house that was a rational, well planned design and not an ostentatious beacon of success. The 3,800 square foot house is a slightly altered L-shaped plan with a large attached garage at the exterior intersection of the two wings.

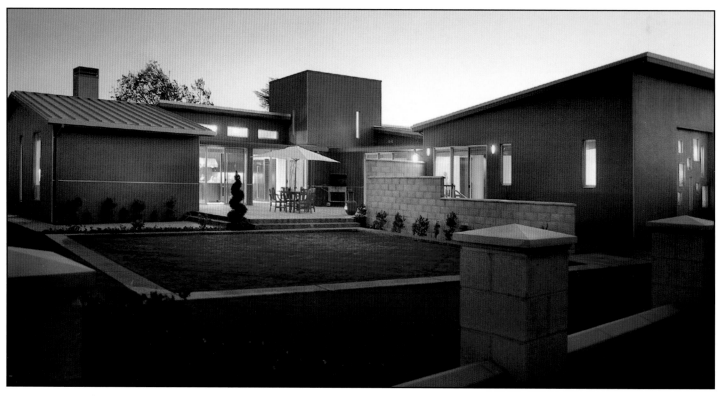

The horizontal configuration is visually enhanced as each house section is delineated with its own distinct form with rooflines recalling the agricultural vernacular of the region. Fenestration patterning varies with narrow vertical windows, sliding glass doors, and clerestory windows throughout the house. A random pattern of fused decorative windows provides diffused natural light near the whirlpool bath. *Courtesy of Avila Design/Yick Kai Chan.*

The house is clad in smooth textured stucco, painted dark brown, and trimmed with medium gray fascias, creating a natural connection to the farming landscape. The butterfly and angled shed roof elements complement each other, and the minimal use of glazing on the western elevation reduces solar heat gain and fulfills the owner's desire for privacy from the adjacent road. *Courtesy of Avila Design/Yick Kai Chan.*

Since the house is fairly close to the front property line, the main entrance is set back 40' beyond the splayed front walls. The covered walkway is reminiscent of the architecture of Eichler homes and Richard Neutra residences. *Courtesy of Avila Design/Yick Kai Chan.*

The interior is composed with circulation hallways of low flat ceilings progressing to public spaces and bedrooms with vaulted ceilings. The dining and kitchen area is a skillful composition of stainless steel, chrome, and granite slab countertops, reflecting the client's main concern that the house be easy and simple to clean. The abundant use of stainless steel throughout the home is a reference to his long career in the sanitary transportation of milk and other perishable liquid foods. *Courtesy of Avila Design/Yick Kai Chan.*

Clerestory windows provide glare-reducing illumination and much needed ventilation in this very warm region of California. The look and feel of the interior resembles many Eichler homes with long low lines and an indoor/outdoor environment provided by sliding glass doors with access to both summer and winter-oriented patios. *Courtesy of Avila Design/Yick Kai Chan.*

The lightly textured warm white walls and maple floors are a pleasing contrast to the dark stained ash veneer on cabinets, door skins, and ceiling planes. The client preferred dark finishes but disliked extreme color variation and contrast. The design team and client were both challenged to find the right combination to strike that perfect balance. *Courtesy of Avila Design/ Yick Kai Chan.*

A random pattern of various size custom-fused glass windows with a falling leaf pattern provide a backdrop on this wall by the whirlpool bath. The rich feel of limestone flooring with these unique north-facing windows creates a peaceful atmosphere for relaxation at any time of day. *Courtesy of Avila Design/Yick Kai Chan*

SMALL AND COZY HOMES

Many of us revel in the idea of the simple cottage or cabin. Perhaps it is from perusing the fairy tales of our childhood, where all sorts of wondrous people inhabited lovely cottages. Perhaps we feel like Thoreau, that cottage life is warm and cheery. Perhaps we just want to downsize, to get away from suburbia or the city and sit on that porch and rock away.

Courtesy of D. Peter Lund.

Courtesy of D. Peter Lund.

Courtesy of Scott Rodwin.

CONTEMPORARY BEACH CABIN

This 1,770 square foot retreat is nestled on one of the last undeveloped waterfront lots in an older beach community on the northeastern shore of Camano Island. Design Northwest Architects created a structure that gives a sense of inner warmth and shelter from the surrounding elements.

View towards the entry.
©*Steve Keating.*

With views to the Cascades and Mt. Baker over Port Susan, this modern-day cabin incorporates traditional elements such as river rock, pine floors, board and batten interior walls, and flat paneled cabinets within its contemporary treatment of space and natural light. ©*Steve Keating.*

The arbor announces entry to the courtyard. Privacy is ensured by a layer of bermed planting areas and defined by a low stonewall culminating in a steel-framed arbor supporting the wisteria. The arbor also frames the view from the second bedroom. ©Steve Keating.

Inside the courtyard, the entry opens up the living space inside, with hints of the beach beyond. ©Steve Keating.

Open interior spaces are achieved through the use of natural glu-lam roof trusses and open beams connected by exposed steel plates and bolting. The windows frame views to the beach or to the courtyard and entry. ©Steve Keating.

The living, dining, and kitchen areas are open to each other, creating a flowing space under a canopy of roof structure. ©*Steve Keating.*

View of kitchen bar. ©*Steve Keating.*

Dining area with views of water and beach. ©*Steve Keating.*

Window seat in dining room. ©*Steve Keating.*

View of dining area from entry ©*Steve Keating.*

Great room ceiling detail.
©Steve Keating.

Skylight in the second bedroom. *©Steve Keating.*

The master suite has no walls separating the bath from the sleeping area. The spa and glass shower are expressed as sculptural objects in an open space. Yellow pine planking runs continuous throughout the suite. Light green ceramic tiles embossed with images of sea life are incorporated into the tile work. The back of the stone fireplace wall is left exposed to the bedroom and bath area. One can shower or bathe while looking out to the beach beyond the sleeping area. The skylight above the spa affords views to the stars at night and allows natural light during the day. *©Steve Keating.*

113

ITTA BITTA HUS

The owners wanted to convert their vacation property in northern Minnesota to a place suitable for retirement. They had always stayed in the "Itta Bitta Hus," their tiny lakeside cabin, when they visited the property, but knew that a larger, more comfortable home would be required to meet their needs in retirement. They also wanted a home that would blend into the lakeside scenery.

They hired Terrasol Restoration & Renovation to build them their dream home, combining two authentic, vintage log cabins, native to the Midwest.

Given their Norwegian heritage, the clients chose an 1860s cabin built by settlers who had immigrated to the United States from Norway. After arriving from Vik, Norway, in 1865, Ingebret Martinson built the Iowa cabin. The three-room floor plan of the cabin is typical of Western Norway. Norwegian style is further indicated by the unusual log gable ends, hand-hewn flat square logs, and dovetailed corners.

Maintaining their cultural tradition and after a month long trip to Norway to visit folk museums, the clients designed their cabin in a traditional Norwegian style. The intent was to finish the building as if Ingebret Martinson had built the same structure in Norway: casement instead of double-hung windows, the wide fascia boards, and flat doors of weathered planks without trim or windows. *Courtesy of Michael E. Miller.*

The main cabin (24' x18') features a full second story, accessed by a winding, custom-built staircase. *Courtesy of Michael E. Miller.*

The stair planks were salvaged from a flour mill in Mankato, Minnesota. *Courtesy of Michael E. Miller.*

The exposed second floor joists running throughout the living room are rustic hand hewn 8" x 8" salvaged barn timbers; the reminiscent mortise-and-tenons and peg holes from the barn construction are still visible. *Courtesy of Michael E. Miller.*

Many of the cabin's decorative touches – the walk out basement door, antique hutch, and family quilt – were inspired by traditional Norwegian style. *Courtesy of Michael E. Miller.*

The addition (18' x 16') is vaulted to give the kitchen a spacious feel. The ceilings in the kitchen and upstairs, the floors, and the gable end siding in the kitchen are made from salvaged barn boards from a turn-of-the-century southern Wisconsin barn. *Courtesy of Michael E. Miller.*

The clients chose decorative fascia to outline the cabin roof. Characteristically Norwegian, the fascia rises above the roofline, extends past the soffits, and hangs below the eaves. In Norway, the oversized fascia was designed to accommodate a sod roof. *Courtesy of Michael E. Miller.*

They also designed a protected porch that created an open overhang to store their outdoor equipment. *Courtesy of Michael E. Miller.*

Located in the tip of a narrow peninsula on Big Sandy Lake, the clients can view the lake from both sides of their new home. The "Itta Bitta Hus" is now a guesthouse, and the clients can't wait to retire! *Courtesy of Michael E. Miller.*

HELL'S CANYON COTTAGE

This tiny 1,200 square foot cottage perches on a small knoll surrounded by 309 pristine acres just outside of Rocky Mountain National Park in Larimer County, Colorado. It sits in a valley, which is the site of a turn-of-the century cattle summer pasture.

Designed by Rodwin Architecture, the cabin features load-bearing straw bale and cementitious plaster walls (R-50+ with a 5-hour fire rating), with a "truth window" (to see the straw bale). It also has an R-38 SIP (structural insulated panel) roof covered with Vermont slate tile; low and non-toxic finishes, sealants, construction adhesives, and stains throughout; partial earth-berming on the North side using Insulated Concrete Forms (ICF), an innova-tive, concrete-reducing (50% less) foundation design (2' spread footer, 8" stem wall with an 18" ledge to support the strawbale wall – instead of the typical full 18" stem wall); engineered lumber floor framing and sheathing; radiant floor heating; both active (photovoltaic array) and passive solar (passive solar orientation and good day-lighting); a super-efficient propane electric back-up; a hand-pump well back-up; dead-standing, locally harvested and milled, beetle-kill lodgepole pine floors, trim, columns, and railings; local mossrock and sandstone walls; recycled cotton batt insulation (between the bedrooms, in the eaves, and in the framed second story walls); low-E, high-efficiency windows; natural wool carpeting; and native revegetation.

This off-the-grid custom residence is a showcase for sustainable design created to be handed down from generation to generation. Its designed lifespan is three hundred years. Created as a mountain retreat for two families, it sleeps up to fourteen people. *Courtesy of Scott Rodwin.*

Rodwin Architecture sited the cottage for optimal passive solar orientation, protection by the hillside from the northwest chilling winds, commanding views of the valley, and minimal grade displacement. *Courtesy of Scott Rodwin.*

It is common on straw bale projects to reveal the unusual nature of the construction by leaving the straw bale wall bare (unplastered) in one spot on the interior wall. Many of these "truth windows" are artistically decorated with picture frames or other elements. At Hell's Canyon, the builder added twigs from the site to form a pleasing and original composition. *Courtesy of Scott Rodwin.*

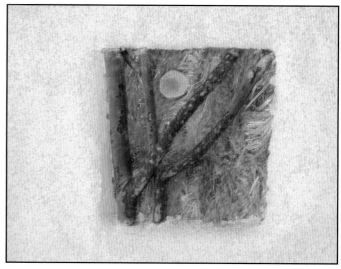

The land is marked by a road gate welded by a neighbor from a turn-of-the-century plow that was found on the property. *Courtesy of Scott Rodwin.*

A sleeping and play loft, resembling a tree house, overlooks the great room. *Courtesy of Juliet Jones Photofolio, Inc.*

This traditional wood-burning Rumford fireplace is surrounded by pink local sandstone. *Courtesy of Juliet Jones Photofolio, Inc.*

This earthy gem has many unique architectural aspects: a cozy bonco (a Mexican/southwestern feature referring to a cave-like nook) filled with pillows is just one of them. *Courtesy of Juliet Jones Photofolio, Inc.*

Artistic, rustic woodwork and custom Alder cabinetry can be found throughout the cabin. *Courtesy of Juliet Jones Photofolio, Inc.*

A wood-dowelled heavy-timber roof framing spans the vaulted great room. *Courtesy of Scott Rodwin.*

A bed and bath. *Courtesy of Juliet Jones Photofolio, Inc.*

The cabin includes a gazebo, poetic eyebrow window and entry gable, copper gutters with chain link downspouts, and a romantic, wood-fired, outdoor cedar hot tub. *Courtesy of Juliet Jones Photofolio, Inc.*

The beautiful and unique bathroom has a cedar-lined two-person shower and a river-rock floor. *Courtesy of Juliet Jones Photofolio, Inc.*

The octagonal gazebo has spectacular 270-degree views of the private valley. *Courtesy of Tim Murphy.*

What a place! *Courtesy of Scott Rodwin.*

LANDSCAPING WORKSHOP TO COZY GAMBREL HOME

This house is located in a tourist town, two miles from the ocean. The original structure, which was on a slab, housed a local landscaping company. Architect Kristi Woloszyn transformed this gambrel workspace into a home that has links to both classic New England style and modern architecture.

The former landscaping company is now a charming three-bedroom, three-bath home. *Courtesy of Kristi Woloszyn, AIA.*

The owner replaced the oversized garage door with French doors and side windows to take advantage of the view of the pond. *Courtesy of Kristi Woloszyn, AIA.*

The galley kitchen opens to the great room with triple windows in the dining area and French doors in the sitting area. A gas fireplace with ceramic tile hearth adds charm and warmth to the cozy space. *Courtesy of Kristi Woloszyn, AIA.*

To allow for plumbing but still maintain the eleven-foot ceiling height in the great room, she raised the first floor bathroom, laundry, and bedroom three feet, creating a crawl space. *Courtesy of Kristi Woloszyn, AIA.*

The windows and doors are trimmed in light wood, which contrasts with the cherry floor. *Courtesy of Kristi Woloszyn, AIA.*

The architect chose warm hues of burnt orange, brick red, and tan for the walls. *Courtesy of Kristi Woloszyn, AIA.*

This guest bath is one of several. *Courtesy of Kristi Woloszyn, AIA.*

BEACHSIDE RETREAT

This retreat is located on the eastern side of Camano Island, with views to the Cascade Mountains. The clients requested that Design Northwest Architects incorporate traditional elements such as wood shingle siding, a natural stone fireplace, and a wood-burning cook stove into a modern aesthetic.

Because the retreat is to be shared by three generations of one family, the plan called for three separate sleeping areas with their own bath areas.

The curved roof allowed enough volume to get the loft in under the maximum volumetric requirements. Tempered glass was used to allow the curved ceiling to be seen from the living room and yet provide acoustic privacy for the loft.

The kitchen, dining, and living areas are considered to be common areas and left open with expansive glass to take in views of the beach and sound. ©*Steve Keating.*

The view of the house from the beach. ©*Steve Keating.*

French doors open out to a large deck area, so that living can be easily taken outside in the summer months. A curved wall of glass off the kitchen orients views to the South down Port Susan Bay. Corner windows in the living room look out toward Mt. Baker. Here can be seen the living room and sleeping loft. ©*Steve Keating.*

Steel stair and rails with maple treads and risers lead up to the loft accessed by a bridge framed with glu-lam beams and 2" x 6" tongue and groove decking. ©*Steve Keating.*

The garage has storage above with a curved roofline to match the roof over the main volume of the house. An angled wall of glass leading from the garage opens up to a view of the entry courtyard on the north. The south wall provides gallery space for family photographs. The south wall of the north bedroom wing gently curves, leading guests into the courtyard and main entry, which has a raised skylight above. The entry door is sheathed in copper to match the copper used throughout the exterior for flashing and drain scuppers. ©Steve Keating.

View to sleeping loft from landing. ©Steve Keating.

The house was built in an area with a 1 1/2 story height restriction, which meant that one of the sleeping areas had to be tucked into the roofline. This view of the sleeping loft looks towards the transom glass and landing. ©Steve Keating.

EXPANDING RETIREMENT COTTAGE

Finding an ideal location for a dream home is the first challenge. Environmental factors and government regulations make it increasingly hard to find and build on property along the water. Moreover, most of the property has been bought up. But it can be done. Over several years, this couple turned a beach cottage into a retirement home.

The water's edge. *Courtesy of D. Peter Lund.*

The cottage decorated for the holiday season.
Courtesy of D. Peter Lund.

The kitchen overlooks the street. *Courtesy of D. Peter Lund.*

At the opposite end of the room is a bar facing the deck and the seawall. *Courtesy of D. Peter Lund.*

The continually changing beauty of the ocean is mesmerizing. *Courtesy of D. Peter Lund.*

On the other hand, the ocean can be destructive. The lumber protects the owner's plants from winter storms. *Courtesy of D. Peter Lund.*

The vent in the overhang protects the roof from back-up leaks from the winter storms. *Courtesy of D. Peter Lund.*

Note the built-in cupboards. *Courtesy of D. Peter Lund.*

A clever place for the kitchen pantry.
Courtesy of D. Peter Lund.

The home office has a wonderful view. *Courtesy of D. Peter Lund.*

The bedrooms draw on the color of the water. *Courtesy of D. Peter Lund.*

Great rooms for the grandchildren.
Courtesy of D. Peter Lund.

This house continues to grow as the family increases. Originally, the owners put plumbing in the attic. Today, it is being revamped as the grandchildren begin to want their own private space. Great storage exists under the eaves. To access it more readily, the owners plan to install doors – with Velcro! *Courtesy of D. Peter Lund.*

Beach Cabin to
Full-Time Residence

The design goal for Design Northwest Architects was to turn a forty year old beach cabin into a full-time residence for a husband and wife, who were just entering retirement.

The waterside deck opens up to the sea breezes and is equipped with a small soaking tub. Because of the limited land area, the southern deck was designed to accommodate raised planting beds for vegetables and herbs. Wisteria will eventually cover the open framework above the deck, further reinforcing this area as the outdoor garden. *Courtesy of Dan Nelson.*

The 1,847 square foot house is entered through an enclosed courtyard, making the transition from the street to the entry alcove. The courtyard also acts as a private outdoor room, with a southern exposure away from the winds off the bay.

The entry alcove is recessed to provide protection from the elements and is defined as a box wrapped in fir board and batten on the interior. *Courtesy of Dan Nelson.*

The cabin sat nine feet away from an existing bulkhead on the waterside and seventeen feet from the road on the other side. Setback restrictions made it necessary to stay within the footprint of the existing structure. *Courtesy of Dan Nelson.*

Once through the glass front door, the interior space is open to the living, kitchen, and dining area and is expressed as a two-story volume with a loft study above. *Courtesy of Dan Nelson.*

Tucked into one corner of the first floor is a studio space that doubles as guest quarters. Because of the small square footage of the house, every space had to be designed for efficiency. A walk-in pantry off the kitchen allows ample storage for kitchen goods, and a built-in library under the stair also provides a computer desk. *Courtesy of Dan Nelson.*

An open stair leads up to the loft/study, creating a transition from the public space to the privacy of the master bedroom. The loft is also an extension of the bedroom, acting as a sitting area for the master suite *Courtesy of Dan Nelson.*

BEACH HOUSE RENOVATION

This beach house sits high above the water at the edge of the Atlantic. E.R. Racek Associates renovated the exterior façade. The owners like to entertain and were concerned that their deck was not safe for large groups. E. R. Racek designed a mahogany deck and railing, which allowed for wonderful parties.

The rail fittings are made from stainless steel. Its thin strands of stainless wire do not obscure or ruin the view from the windows.

Part of the deck is cantilevered from a center column, which radiates beams to support the outer points of the deck. At night, it is lit from underneath, which gives a radiant glow—particularly when you are sipping some wine. The hard wood will stand up to the abuse of the ocean. The only maintenance is a yearly spraying of a water repellent to help preserve the deck from the ocean salts and the sun.

Because of the beautiful setting, Racek designed the deck bigger than normal. As a result, it becomes an extension of the house. The different levels of the deck allow for different seating areas and provide space for dining, conversation, and just gazing at the ever-changing ocean.

HOUSE ON THOMPSON RAVINE CREEK

The Wells Barn was ready to retire. Mark Johnson of Terrasol Restoration & Renovation decided to give this regal symbol of the Midwestern landscape a new lease on life. His crew and he dismantled the hand hewn timber frame, mapped and tagged the timbers, and transported it to their storage site.

In 2004, Terrasol Restoration reconstructed the barn as a vacation home on a quiet creek. The new home has a full basement and 2/3 loft. The main floor is designed with an open concept kitchen and dining room exposed to the vaulted great room.

The custom built staircase features one hundred year-old salvaged floor joists from a flour mill from Amboy, Minnesota. *Courtesy of Michael E. Miller.*

Rustic log bridge across the Thompson Ravine Creek. *Courtesy of Michael E. Miller.*

The vaulted great room features one hundred seven year-old timbers, log mantle, and a custom staircase with glass panel railing. The 26' x 46' timber frame home was built from the better half of a 96' x 46' barn built in 1898 near Wells, Minnesota. The large size of the barn meant that the timbers were oversized as well. The 10" x 10" posts and beams are visible throughout the home. These rough sawn timbers were hand planed before assembly. *Courtesy of Michael E. Miller.*

The glass railing allows light to permeate the open loft area. *Courtesy of Michael E. Miller.*

The open concept kitchen and dining room keep the cook happy. *Courtesy of Michael E. Miller.*

The fireplace and the mantle are the highlight of the great room. *Courtesy of Michael E. Miller.*

The master bedroom has a private view of the ravine. *Courtesy of Michael E. Miller.*

The master bedroom has a whirlpool tub where the owners can hear the creek flowing just outside the bathroom window. *Courtesy of Michael E. Miller.*

A view from the loft. The hardwood floors throughout the main floor accentuate the authentic barn timbers. *Courtesy of Michael E. Miller.*

THE HAPPY MEDIUM

Then there are those homes that offer fine design details and craftsmanship, where their owners can escape from their everyday lives to the golf complex, the tennis court, the waterfront, and the woods… or just to the porch.

Courtesy of D. Peter Lund.

Courtesy of D. Peter Lund.

Courtesy of D. Peter Lund.

Courtesy of D. Peter Lund.

LAKEFRONT HOME

This lakefront home is the fruit of a great deal of owner review along with a rapid deployment of resources, including Tony Fallon Architecture. The foundation was poured while construction drawings were still being drawn.

The hearth is the center of the home. The arched hearth of the rusticated stone mass invites staring, gazing, and conking out in the warmth of the look and flame.

The hearth is wrapped with a curved stair. Halfway up the stairs, the view of the lake breaks through the chimney with a gothic arched opening. *Courtesy of Tony Fallon.*

An infant's view of the fireplace and chimney. The living room couches view both the two-story fireplace and the lake. This move solves a common angst about placing the fireplace on the outside view wall and taking away windows. *Courtesy of Tony Fallon.*

From the balcony at the top of the stairs, you can look over the living and dining rooms and across to the beautiful scull that the owner rows. The joy of and love for rowing is reflected in the paddle railing that Julie Fergus ASID designed. The undulating lakeside wall with playful and plentiful windows enables the light and beauty of the outside to dance inside. *Courtesy of Tony Fallon.*

The kitchen, living, and dining are all the same room distinguished by niches, bays, lights, and heights. The husband designed and built the butcher block island with open shelves. It fits and floats well. Stone faced on all sides, the chimney is the timeless pivot point for these combined rooms. *Courtesy of Tony Fallon.*

The kitchen portion was beyond the original cottage footprint. Since it wasn't grandfathered, it needed to be further back from the lake. This well-windowed kitchen makes a delightful place for creating meals. Storage is accommodated with a pantry back towards the entry and wall cabinets on the roadside wall. The island, designed and constructed by the owner, stores some plates too. The wicker couch is the umpteenth invitation to rest. *Courtesy of Tony Fallon.*

Although the old cottage could not be saved, the desire for the relaxed, comforting, and traditional cottage style remained. In the guest room, light from the cathedral space is gained through both the open door and the interior diamond window. The simple twist of the windows forty-five degrees is a classic country and cottage game. *Courtesy of Tony Fallon.*

The master bedroom is itself a beautiful bay window with wainscoting on the lower wall and radiating around the ceiling. *Courtesy of Tony Fallon.*

A paddle-edged balcony connects the rooms on the second floor with the curved stair while two glass sea gulls eye the scene. The scull floats in the cathedral ceiling with the lake rippling beyond. *Courtesy of Tony Fallon.*

Views from as many portions as possible led to punching a hole in the chimney mass, which permits lake views from the back of the chimney from the winding stair. *Courtesy of Tony Fallon.*

The house meanders along the lakefront affording panoramic viewing and better connection to the outside. The two-story living room is covered with a shed roof interrupted by two steep gables. Bright colors add to the joyful facade. *Courtesy of Tony Fallon.*

From the lake, the right bay of the study and master bedroom stack to make a tower. On the left is the kitchen. The living and dining room gables have high windows, and the stone chimney peeks out of the ridge. *Courtesy of Tony Fallon.*

You enter through an air lock vestibule acting as a decompression chamber. Here, the boots, coats, and other items of the journey can be stowed, and the swirling winter winds kept at bay. *Courtesy of Tony Fallon.*

The entrance to the home focuses on the many views of the lake and brings you into the central hub. *Courtesy of Tony Fallon.*

SUNSHINE EVERY DAY

Venice, Florida, is one of the few cities on the West Coast where the soft white sand beaches of the Gulf of Mexico form the western boundary. Many vacation here; even more retire here, so they can enjoy sunbathing, fishing, swimming and boating along the fourteen miles of beaches.

Just one of the many condo buildings.
Courtesy of D. Peter Lund.

The lanai is at one end of the condo.
Courtesy of D. Peter Lund.

It looks out on the lovely rustling palms.
Courtesy of D. Peter Lund.

The living room is rarely used because there is that big beautiful beach directly outside. *Courtesy of D. Peter Lund.*

The guest bedroom is also the study. Another bedroom and TV area are upstairs, and there is a lovely master suite. *Courtesy of D. Peter Lund.*

Florida is a popular retirement spot. *Courtesy of D. Peter Lund.*

Because there is that great big beautiful outdoors. *Courtesy of D. Peter Lund.*

HOUSE ON THE WATER

Moskow Architects renovated this home by opening up rooms to beautiful outdoor views, adding sculptural space within, redesigning the kitchen, and adding a new master suite and office tower.

The design also incorporates custom stainless steel pieces designed by the architect and fabricated by the client in China. One component is a column capitol shaped after a Chinese cleaver. A second component is the railing stanchions modeled on the abstract form of the Chinese character for sword.

Placing the fireplace in front of the windows allows you to enjoy the fire and the view concurrently. Copyright Greg Premru.

The towers in this house lay shining in the sunlight like a broken mirror. *Copyright Greg Premru.*

The many windows in this vacation-to-retirement home let in the precious sunlight—something you want when on vacation or in retirement. *Copyright Greg Premru*

Space flows freely between the rooms. *Copyright Greg Premru.*

The efficient kitchen is a hostess' dream. *Copyright Greg Premru.*

Storage is everywhere, which is important in a vacation-to-retirement house, which may be used by others. *Copyright Greg Premru.*

The railing does not obstruct the view. *Copyright Greg Premru.*

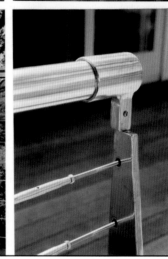

Poets would love this view. *Copyright Greg Premru.*

CAPE COMPONENT HOUSE

Moskow Architects added a semi-transparent "library tower" to this house. The tower connects a 1950s cape cottage to a new (2001) cape counterpart designed to mimic the original. A glass box piano room protrudes from the new structure, breaking from the building envelope and from cape house tradition.

The newly renovated house makes a bold statement. *Copyright Greg Premru.*

Here, you can see the old cape cottage. *Copyright Greg Premru.*

The house at night is striking. *Copyright Greg Premru.*

Although the total habitable space is only 2,400 square feet, the tower transforms this cape. *Copyright Greg Premru.*

The glassbox piano room not only breaks from the building envelope but is a great place to hear your favorite piano music. *Copyright Greg Premru.*

The kitchen is long and sleek. *Copyright Greg Premru.*

The open stairway. *Copyright Greg Premru.*

An exterior view of the stairway. *Copyright Greg Premru.*

159

SEPARATE GUEST SUITES

Design Northwest Architects carefully placed this house on a long and narrow slot of land between the waterfront setback and the drain field on the roadside.

The firm's approach was to orient the house to the water with entry, living, dining, and family space flowing together, opening up to a two-story space. The master suite and den were designed apart from the main living area, allowing the client to maintain privacy even while entertaining family and friends.

The second floor is devoted to guest bedrooms and divided into separate suites so two separate sets of guests can visit and have relative privacy.

View from the great room towards water. ©*Steve Keating.*

The client requested a classic design that looked as though it had always been there. It was built with shingle, river rock, wood beams, and decking on the inside. Shingles were applied to the overhead garage door so it would blend in with the house. The client did not want to drive up to an obvious garage door. ©*Steve Keating.*

Because of heavy afternoon winds from the northwest, the clients requested a screened sitting area on the entry side – out of the wind for relaxing. Design Northwest Architects achieved this by the use of latticed arbors that also frame the entry. ©*Steve Keating.*

Master bathroom.
©*Steve Keating.*

A covered deck on the waterside becomes an extension of the house, using the same framing and color scheme as the interior ceiling. ©*Steve Keating.*

View from dining area of great room and bridge. ©*Steve Keating.*

View of stairway to loft. Halogen lights were placed up in the trusses to highlight the ceiling, a concern to the client. The halogens are unobtrusive in the structure. Additionally, the ceiling was painted to lighten the interior. Warm glow fluorescent light coffers were placed over window walls. ©*Steve Keating.*

The water view of the exterior. ©*Steve Keating.*

163

WILDERNESS CONTEMPORARY DESIGN

Here, among the pines and the birches, the bears amble about, deer frolic, and an occasional moose walks across the property. This couple had a picture of the ideal house, but needed interior design advice. They found the land and visited an architect with their ideas and the picture. He designed their ideal home.

The land. *Courtesy of D. Peter Lund.*

When you retire, you may want the grandchildren to come visit. These grandchildren have their playhouse. *Courtesy of D. Peter Lund.*

He built the gazebo for his wife so she could watch (bug-free) the construction of the house. *Courtesy of D. Peter Lund.*

You need a hammock on a porch like this. *Courtesy of D. Peter Lund.*

The dream house overlooks the valley. *Courtesy of D. Peter Lund.*

The loft, porch, and bedroom have cathedral ceilings. *Courtesy of D. Peter Lund.*

The owner had always wanted a fieldstone fireplace. The rocks for it came from selectively selecting rocks off the old walls on the property. *Courtesy of D. Peter Lund.*

The living room has a breathtaking panoramic view. *Courtesy of D. Peter Lund.*

The house contains important family memorabilia and antiques. *Courtesy of D. Peter Lund.*

The kitchen opens to the living and dining room. *Courtesy of D. Peter Lund.*

The bedrooms are resplendent with the owner's quilts and samplers. *Courtesy of D. Peter Lund.*

The master bedroom closets are fitted with small children's beds for the grandchildren. *Courtesy of D. Peter Lund.*

She always wanted a tower.
Courtesy of D. Peter Lund.

Both like stained glass.
Courtesy of D. Peter Lund.

Both like the view from the tower. *Courtesy of D. Peter Lund.*

And all around them are the beautiful woods. *Courtesy of D. Peter Lund.*

MERCER ISLAND
NORTH RESIDENCE

Surrounded by amazing natural beauty, Mercer Island, Washington, is in the middle of scenic Lake Washington. The Cascade Mountains are to the east; the Olympic range is to the west. The island has quiet, treed neighborhoods with city, mountain, and waterfront views.

The island has three hundred-plus acres of parklands and recreational space, including fields, bike trails, and picnic areas. In addition, there are more than fifty miles of marked walking trails.

This residence, designed by Thielsen Architects Inc. P.S. and built by Paulsen Construction Inc. emphasizes simplicity and understated detailing in its interpretation of the Shingle style. It is located just ten feet away from a public park.

The warm-hued stained Alder cabinets, soap stone countertops, and the stainless steel appliances complement the slate flooring. The use of these materials accentuates the importance of natural elements throughout the house. ©www.steve-keating.com

The natural stone walls of the base provide privacy for the house, while the wooden upper floors are open to the views and the natural light. ©www.steve-keating.com.

The living room, which seems expansive and open during the day, feels cozy and intimate in the evening light. Candle sconces paint the fireplace wall with strokes of light and shadow highlighting the recessed panels. ©*www.steve-keating.com*

The wood-fired pizza oven is a focal point for entertaining and an active part of the cooking area of the kitchen. The pantry beyond serves as both a storage area and an interior potting area. ©*www.steve-keating.com*

The finely crafted white painted millwork of the living room contrasts elegantly with the dark mahogany floors. The even north light that fills the space accentuates the details of the coffered ceiling. ©*www.steve-keating.com*

LAKESIDE VIEWS

We spend a lot of our lives pulled into vortexes of televisions, computers, and windshields. This charming design by Tony Fallon Architecture does not have these myopic flat front walls. Instead, the lakeside of this vacation home is faceted to enable broad appreciation of the beauties of creation.

The home is set at a forty-five degree angle to the lake, and so the entry, which aligns with a view axis to the lake through the living room, must be on the corner of the home. Not the standard cape here. *Courtesy of Tony Fallon.*

The living, dining, and porch are all down a couple of steps. The living room is open to the kitchen and looks through windows to the screened porch. The kitchen is fitted with many windows and is open to the lower dining area. *Courtesy of Tony Fallon.*

The driveway loops at the end near the front door. The home radiates out from the entry taking advantage of the views up and down the lake, which was a major wish of the owner. *Courtesy of Tony Fallon.*

Entering the house brings a view through the slightly lower living room to the lake. To the left is the master suite and stairs to the loft. Around the corner to the right of the coat cabinet is the hall to the kitchen and dining. *Courtesy of Tony Fallon.*

To the left of the stairs at the top is a loft for children to rattle around in. *Courtesy of Tony Fallon.*

This balcony leads the guests graciously to their rooms. To the left of the stairs is the open loft. *Courtesy of Tony Fallon.*

The master bedroom, like the rest of the home, is on a forty-five degree angle to the lake, allowing views up and down the lake. This wonderful room is just the right size with great vistas and a romantic fireplace. *Courtesy of Tony Fallon.*

CAPE COD LIFESTYLE

This personal sanctuary is tucked into the scenic wooded Cape. It looks out on the beautiful woods, the pretty gardens, and eye-filling sunsets through dramatic walls of glass.

Designed primarily by the owner, this timeless house overlooks the water. *Courtesy of D. Peter Lund.*

The gardens remain lovely – even in December. *Courtesy of D. Peter Lund.*

Even from the front of the house, you can see the water. *Courtesy of D. Peter Lund.*

The living room is flooded with the light. *Courtesy of D. Peter Lund.*

This is the house of an antique lover, who loves her family. *Courtesy of D. Peter Lund.*

The dining room is in the front of the house. *Courtesy of D. Peter Lund.*

The party-perfect kitchen overlooks the water and the deck. *Courtesy of D. Peter Lund.*

The deck sprawls over the water. *Courtesy of D. Peter Lund.*

At the other end of the house is a lovely den, which could be turned into a downstairs bedroom, if necessary. *Courtesy of D. Peter Lund.*

Just one of the several bedrooms. *Courtesy of D. Peter Lund.*

From the front hall, you can see the shed that holds all the equipment necessary for many guests. *Courtesy of D. Peter Lund.*

The upstairs hall is lined with bookcases. *Courtesy of D. Peter Lund.*

A BARN TO FIT
THEIR LIFESTYLE

In their search for a retirement home in New Hampshire, this couple looked at nearly twenty homes, including five or six Yankee Barns. They realized building was the only way to have their wish list.

Yankee Barn prides itself on helping homeowners turn their ideas into the home they want. The couple brought their sketches to the firm. The firm developed their ideas into plans, helped site the house to take advantage of the views and gain southern exposure in the winter, and incorporated new ideas along the way.

Barn homes provide the warmth of antique wood and the strength of timber frame. *Courtesy of ©Suki Coughlin/Paula McFarland Stylist.*

Usually, they have large open living areas. *Courtesy of ©Suki Coughlin/ Paula McFarland Stylist.*

And adjoining intimate spaces framed in post. A barn home can create a feeling of permanence and a connection to the land as it blends into the environment. *Courtesy of ©Suki Coughlin/Paula McFarland Stylist.*

The porch. *Courtesy of ©Suki Coughlin/ Paula McFarland Stylist.*

PERFECT SITE

A couple found the perfect site to build their vacation-to-retirement home: it was surrounded by farmland with a natural slope down to a lake. Yankee Barn helped them to position their home so they could see the lake from multiple aspects in the house, and visitors could see the house from the driveway and from the water.

The U.S. Environmental Protection Agency (EPA) awarded this home with the EPA Energy Star for at least 30% less energy use for heating, cooling, and water healing than comparable homes.

The Yankee Barn panel construction causes this energy efficiency level. High performance insulation is combined with the seal "tongue and groove" connection between the panels, which stops air infiltration.

From the distance, the simple clean lines of two buildings at an angle resemble the rambling barn design seen in Maine, Massachusetts, New Hampshire, and Vermont – states where the snow can be several feet deep and the winter wind fierce. Known as continuous architecture, this structure turns corners, runs in lines, and can even dart off at an angle. The farmer can walk from house to barn and be sheltered from the winter's storms. Here, this home is big enough for several families. *Courtesy of ©Suki Coughlin/Paula McFarland Stylist.*

This retirement home has the old world charm of post and beam construction with new modern conveniences. *Courtesy of ©Suki Coughlin/Paula McFarland Stylist.*

Taking advantage of the lay of the land, the house is sited on a slight rise to provide the best views of the lake from the front rooms. The wrap-around porch helps to create a Victorian cottage appearance. *Courtesy of ©Suki Coughlin/Paula McFarland Stylist.*

Traditional barn designs inspired a cupola and carriage barn trim on the standard automatic garage doors. *Courtesy of ©SukiCoughlin/Paula McFarland Stylist.*

181

The homeowners decorated their home using treasures, antique furniture, and "found" materials. Reclaimed Georgia pine was used for the floorboards for the first floor. The living room wainscoting was fabricated from coal bins found in a relative's basement. *Courtesy of ©Suki Coughlin/Paula McFarland Stylist.*

Adjacent to the kitchen, the dining room area is the focal point of the open floor plan. The stone fireplace, 10' raised ceilings, and French doors with the wrap-around porch were ideas the homeowners incorporated after seeing other Yankee Barn homes. *Courtesy of ©Suki Coughlin/ Paula McFarland Stylist.*

The bedroom retains that country feeling. *Courtesy of ©Suki Coughlin/Paula McFarland Stylist.*

The house uses a geo-thermal heat and air conditioning system. The homeowners find that the house is so well insulated that even when they turn down the thermostat when they were away, the house temperature does not drop. *Courtesy of ©Suki Coughlin/Paula McFarland Stylist.*

When young visitors get noisy, you can send them to the loft. *Courtesy of ©Suki Coughlin/Paula McFarland Stylist.*

NEW ADDITION

This couple wanted to expand their home and work with the lay of the land. They worked with the Yankee Barn designers, who ensured that everything flowed from one space to the next.

The new addition fits in with the old house perfectly. *Courtesy of Rich Frutchey.*

The spacious great room permits family gatherings. *Courtesy of Rich Frutchey.*

The size of the kitchen was doubled. From the new kitchen, the cook can be a part of the activity. *Courtesy of Rich Frutchey.*

A master bedroom suite. *Courtesy of Rich Frutchey.*

The kids can escape to the playroom. *Courtesy of Rich Frutchey.*

And a balcony. *Courtesy of Rich Frutchey.*

SALTBOX RETIREMENT

Yankee Barn's web site allows you to select design features, including square footage, number of bedrooms, location of the great room and master bedroom, beam style and stair color, window and door styles, plus exterior and interior finishes.

This client wanted a traditional New England style house. When she saw the Gillie saltbox designed by Yankee Barn, she knew she wanted this barn that looked like a colonial saltbox yet had an open living area and traditional layout.

The interior was modified to fit the client's needs. *Courtesy of Rich Frutchey.*

The exterior resembles a traditional saltbox with clapboard siding and colonial style windows. *Courtesy of Rich Frutchey.*

The large open room for the kitchen and dining area serves as the center of the home. *Courtesy of Rich Frutchey.*

The living room does not have a cathedral ceiling. It retains a cozy feel. *Courtesy of Rich Frutchey.*

There are three bedrooms upstairs. *Courtesy of Rich Frutchey.*

INNOVATIVE
MOUNTAINSIDE RETIREMENT

Topsider Homes integrates post and beam technology with almost any foundation type, making its homes adaptable to nearly any terrain, climate, or need. Its post and beam building system does not rely on interior or exterior load-bearing walls because the large post and beam timbers shoulder the loads. The result is a building system that allows design flexibility, including floor-to-ceiling windows, detailed finishes and upgrade finishes, without sacrificing structural integrity. Its stability against natural forces such as earthquakes, hurricanes, and heavy snow is extraordinary.

Designed with plenty of deck space, this Topsider Home fits snugly into the steep hillside. The pedestal design foundation allows minimal disturbance to the natural landscape. *Courtesy of Topsider.*

Informal decks are literally set in the trees. *Courtesy of Topsider.*

A dramatic view from a formal dining room.
Courtesy of Topsider.

APARTMENT TRANSFORMATION

Currently, the owners of this dwelling live in South America and use this apartment as a vacation-to-retirement home. They requested that Victoria Benatar transform the two-bedroom apartment into a three-bedroom apartment with an eat-in kitchen. They plan to retire here eventually.

The flexibility of the space allows multiple family members to be together at the same time or one family member to invite friends to enjoy the Florida weather.

When you enter this apartment, you immediately notice the view. *Courtesy of Henry Grunberg.*

The living room is entered through a double-door entry. *Courtesy of Henry Grunberg.*

191

Setting the TV and bar into the wall provide more floor space. *Courtesy of Henry Grunberg.*

The white, wooden blinds create a tropical atmosphere to the complement the interior. *Courtesy of Henry Grunberg.*

Art surrounds you everywhere. *Courtesy of Henry Grunberg.*

SOMETHING UNIQUE

Some want something different than just a house. They want a community. Whether it is an on-the-go lifestyle for the still young at heart, a community abroad, or premier golf course living, we have many possibilities.

Courtesy of D. Peter Lund.

Courtesy of D. Peter Lund.

Courtesy of D. Peter Lund.

GOLF RETIREMENT COMMUNITY

Retirement communities are a popular choice for active adults seeking to enjoy those golden years. Many individuals look forward to recreational activities and focus on active adult communities. These developments offer tennis, swimming, and other options for exercise close to home. Increasingly, aging baby boomers are interested in golf retirement communities and want to be on or near a course that they can access at any time.

Privately owned, Penn National grew from a 526-acre farm that traces back to the family of the founder of Chambersburg and a land grant from William Penn Jr. in 1773. In 1967, a group of investors bought the farm and opened the county's first eighteen hole golf course in 1968. By 1970, the group started building homes around the course, preserving a c.1840 manor house to become part of the Penn National Inn.

Over the years, the group acquired more land and added another golf course. Families of all ages live here, but about seventy percent or more are retirees primarily from the metropolitan Baltimore and Washington, DC areas, New York, and New Jersey.

Surrounded by rolling hills, this active community bills itself as a weekend home that a family can enjoy year around. The Appalachian Trail offers hiking and nature; nearby Falling Springs provides good fishing. *Courtesy of Penn National Golf Course Community.*

People who live here like the outdoors. They hike, bike, play golf on the two highly ranked golf courses, fly fish, and ski. *Courtesy of Penn National Golf Course Community.*

The community sits in the middle of the dairy farmland with grazing cows, but it is only two hours away from Washington D.C. *Courtesy of Penn National Golf Course Community.*

Twenty-five thousand homes are planned for the 1,100 acres. About one third have been built and sold. The lots back up to the mountains and state forest, which has forty miles of Appalachian Trail running through it. *Courtesy of Penn National Golf Course Community.*

A number of buyers are investing in real estate and securing retirement since there are no time restrictions to build. New homeowners may purchase a floor plan or bring their own. *Courtesy of Penn National Golf Course Community.*

The homes range from 1,400 square feet with the average being about 2,200 square feet. Most lots are about one-third of an acre. Modern brick guest lodges surround the Manor House, providing spacious guest rooms. *Courtesy of Penn National Golf Course Community.*

Rural tranquility exists in this community, but residents and guests are offered a wide array of activities and amenities. There is the outside heated clubhouse pool, the fully stocked golf shop, the tennis courts, and the clubhouse restaurant. *Courtesy of Penn National Golf Course Community.*

Penn National features two 18-hole championship golf courses – the Founders Course and the Iron Forge. Both courses continue to receive accolades from publications like *Golf Digest* and *Washington Golf Monthly*. The Founders Course features a classic blend of tree-lined fairways, large greens, sculpted bunkers, and a seven-acre lake, while the new Iron Forge Course provides a modern links with sculpted bent-grass fairways more open to the forces of nature. *Courtesy of Penn National Golf Course Community.*

A Geodesic Dome

Housing technology has changed very little since framing replaced the log cabin. Modifications have been made to improve efficiency and strength, but they have also increased cost. Noted architect Buckminster Fuller proved that geodesic domes get stronger, lighter, and cheaper per unit of volume as their size increases – just the opposite of conventional buildings. Reinforced concrete dome home shells are able to withstand enormous wind and snow loads and are fully capable of supporting earth beaming.

An American Ingenuity dome is purchased as a shell kit. Purchasers without prior construction experience can build their own dome, or an independent subcontractor can assemble the dome shell. The simplified building process consists of placing a row of panels, overlapping and interlocking the steel mesh from adjacent panels, and filling the seams with a specially formulated concrete.

High vaulted ceilings are a natural for domes. The strength of the dome is sufficient to suspend the second floor, eliminating the need for load bearing walls and allowing for large open floor areas. Reduced surface area, uninterrupted insulation, lower air infiltration, and expanded polystyrene (EPS) insulation (four times thicker than that used in refrigerators) provide savings in heating and air conditioning cost that often exceed fifty percent.

This forty foot, two thousand square foot dome home has three bedrooms and two baths. It is connected to a thirty foot, two-car garage dome with a half bath, utility area, and second floor. The dome home contains a see-through fireplace, kitchen with an island, sunken living room, sunken tub, and a spacious three hundred forty square foot master bedroom. *Courtesy of American Ingenuity.*

This rear view depicts a thirty-four foot diameter, seven hundred square foot screen dome attached to the house dome. The screen dome encloses the second floor balcony and a first floor entryway. Standard sliding and French doors or windows are installed at other entrances. The second floor of the larger domes can have up to five balconies. *Courtesy of American Ingenuity.*

The skylights provide abundant natural lighting for the entrance and kitchen area. Two layers of thick tempered glass make the skylights strong and energy efficient. Cupolas provide lighting and ventilation and may offer a third floor loft with a 360-degree view. *Courtesy of American Ingenuity.*

The master bath on the second floor has a ten foot mirror and a skylight above the sunken tub. *Courtesy of American Ingenuity.*

Sliding glass doors, twelve feet wide, open from the dining area into the screen dome. *Courtesy of American Ingenuity.*

The second floor balcony offers a private area connected to the master bedroom. Screen domes can enclose a hot tub, swimming pool, vegetable garden, or whatever the homeowner desires. *Courtesy of American Ingenuity.*

The floor plan joins the sunken living room, dining room, kitchen, and entry into a large open area. Kitchen lighting filters down through crystal glasses suspended above the island. Appliance garages line the back of the kitchen counter. The see-through fireplace can also be viewed from a cozy niche on the other side. An open, contemporary single beam staircase leads to the private office and master bedroom above. *Courtesy of American Ingenuity.*

When inside the screen dome, you can look up to the second floor balcony. *Courtesy of American Ingenuity.*

The master bedroom opens up into the cupola loft with windows on all five sides. Through the mirrored closet doors, you can see the king size bed and overhead skylights. *Courtesy of American Ingenuity.*

THE CITY LOFT

Although the usual concept is to purchase a home in the country at retirement, many people return to the city. There, they may be able to eliminate the car and rely on their own feet, a bike, or public transit with the occasional rental vehicle. The symphony or the museum is just blocks away. The restaurants beckon, and the grandchildren will love to visit once they are older.

This apartment, renovated by Anne-Sophie Divenyi and Rupinder Singh, is in the heart of Boston's picturesque Back Bay neighborhood. Fenway Park, the Museum of Fine Arts, Symphony Hall, fashionable Newbury Street, Copley Place, and Boston Common are just some of the sights easily accessible from this condominium.

Counter details. *Courtesy of Doug Cogger.*

The living room and kitchen is the core of this ultra-compact, visually stunning apartment. This apartment offers modern elegance with generous functionality. An extensive number of custom cabinets accomplish a multitude of functions with visual grace. *Courtesy of Doug Cogger.*

Compact urban spaces spark design creativity by accommodating multiple functions with a single object. Two identical rolling tables are docked within the kitchen base cabinets for day-to-day functions. *Courtesy of Anne-Sophie Divenyi.*

For special occasions, these tables can be rolled out to transform into separate or paired end tables. They can be combined with a removable leaf into a dining table that seats six comfortably. Guests are literally invited to help the host "set" the table! *Courtesy of Doug Cogger.*

The juxtaposition of a ten foot sliding translucent/clear door and generous built-in shelving elaborates the tension between storage and display – a motif explored throughout the design. The metal trim is a crisp articulation of the fluid public and private areas. *Courtesy of Anne-Sophie Divenyi.*

What is revealed can also be obfuscated. In the twilight hours, the translucent panels become more reflective and opaque. Where they once created openness and permeated light, they now subtly control light and view. Framed moments are introduced in the clear sections of the panels, thereby hinting at activity beyond immediate sight. *Courtesy of Doug Cogger.*

The bedroom is integral to the loft style pied-a-terre experience. Translucent sliding panels both separate and connect living and resting spaces in this condominium. Built-in shelving allows for an elegant display and storage system. *Courtesy of Doug Cogger.*

Push open a translucent door and enter a world of storage. All city dwellers envy generous yet discrete storage: shelving, roll-out cabinets, hanging rods, a drop down ironing table, even cubbies for clothes, knick-knacks, or hair wear! *Courtesy of Doug Cogger.*

A custom bathroom vanity is the ultimate luxury in a small city dwelling. The cabinet is gener-ously proportioned for ample internal storage, steel legs allow for visual lightness, and a graceful bowl sink completes the composition. *Courtesy of Anne-Sophie Divenyi.*

No pied-a-terre is complete without a spectacular view. The apartment commands a pristine view across the Charles River to the MIT campus. An annual activity is watching the July 4th fireworks display with friends and family. *Courtesy of Doug Cogger.*

SONG OF THE OPEN ROAD

Walt Whitman said in his poem:

> I think heroic deeds were all conceived in the open
> air, and all free poems also,
> I think I could stop here myself and do miracles,
> I think whatever I shall meet on the road I shall
> like,
> and whoever beholds me shall like me,
> I think whoever I see must be happy.

That wide open road always encourages us to explore what lies just beyond the horizon. In an RV, you can see new places and make new friends. You can get away from it all and not adhere to others' deadlines.

Camping with the kids and weekend getaways can easily change to full-time retirement in an RV. You can explore the Unites States, travel to Alaska, visit the historic sites (or the racetracks), and check out the nation's wineries.

You don't have to worry about making the trip to the airport or checking out by 11:00AM. You don't have to make a reservation for the next motel or find a good place for dinner. If you don't like where you are, you can move on. In an RV, everything you need is within a few feet.

An RV gives you the flexibility to go where you want. *Courtesy of D. Peter Lund.*

From sea to shining sea, the United States has immense reaches of grasslands, lakes, rivers, farms, forests, and mountains. In this RV, you can explore them for months. *Courtesy of D. Peter Lund.*

It also has the navigational aids that ensure that you will get there. *Courtesy of D. Peter Lund.*

Your co-pilot has easy access to the back of the vehicle here. A TV up front and in the master bedroom ensures you stay in touch with the world. There's even a recliner chair on the far right. *Courtesy of D. Peter Lund.*

A fully self-contained RV with shower toilet, kitchen, TV, couches, and beds can be quite luxurious. The dining room transforms into a bed for your guests. *Courtesy of D. Peter Lund.*

If you own an RV, you can eat at "home" or in that really nice-looking restaurant. *Courtesy of D. Peter Lund.*

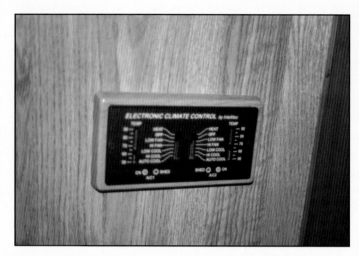

The HVAC system allows the owner to keep their home as warm or as cool as they like. *Courtesy of D. Peter Lund.*

The refrigerator is big enough to contain your food, chill your wine, and maybe a six-pack too! *Courtesy of D. Peter Lund.*

The kitchen has everything you need. *Courtesy of D. Peter Lund.*

You don't have to find the local Laundromat either. *Courtesy of D. Peter Lund.*

A traffic jam doesn't create that bathroom crisis, and the bathroom is always clean! *Courtesy of D. Peter Lund.*

RV owners can sleep in their own bed on their favorite mattress brand. They also can watch TV in bed too. *Courtesy of D. Peter Lund.*

OVER THE BOUNDING MAIN

At those high school and college reunions, you always run into one or two couples who have decided to sell their homes and explore the world's waterways when they retire.

Sabre sailing yachts offer a blend of cruising comfort and racing performance. They are available in lengths from 38' to 45' and have high load carrying capacities. Sabre keels are designed for maximum lift and solid performances. Sail plans are created with both light winds and harsh weather in mind. The Sabre 426 won *Sail Magazine's* Top Ten award.

The Sabre 452 was voted Best Full-Size Cruiser (41'-47') for 1998 by *Cruising World Magazine. Courtesy of Sabre Yachts.*

Sabre sailing yachts are designed to be performance cruising yachts, blending the comfort of cruising, with a capacity for blue water passage making. They are capable of competitive racing and winning club regattas. *Courtesy of Sabre Yachts.*

Standard yachts have Sabre White hulls and decks with varnished cherry interiors. *Courtesy of Sabre Yachts.*

Its motor yacht line is a development of the style and comfort of the traditional "down east style" yacht blended with the performance of a contemporary motor yacht. Typical cruising speeds, with average weight conditions and sea state, are in the twenty-knot range, and top speeds, with average load conditions are around thirty knots. Higher speeds are available on some specific models. *Courtesy of Sabre Yachts.*

At low engine speeds, the Sabreline range is very fuel efficient and at speeds of eight to ten knots, where typical trawler yachts operate, low speed gunk holing is a pleasure. But when conditions or time allow for higher speed, the performance of the Sabreline deep-vee hulls come into their own. In rough sea conditions, the spray rails and chines of the Sabreline hull keep the deck and windshield dry. *Courtesy of Sabre Yachts.*

This motor yacht offers modern hull lines, higher cruise speeds, more space for today's sophisticated navigational technology, and more space to relax and enjoy your time on the water. *Courtesy of Sabre Yachts.*

COLLABORATION BETWEEN
THE DECORATOR AND THE CLIENT

—Charlene Keogh, Keogh Design, New York, New York

This apartment on the upper east side of Manhattan is the dream home of Ted and Marianne Hovivian, who moved to Manhattan after raising three children on Long Island. They had looked for years before finding their dream place.

They found this apartment, which was originally created for a family member of the building's owner. They then asked Charlene Keogh, the owner of Keogh Design Inc., to design it.

The condominium encompasses half the floor plan of the building – over what would have been two apartments. As a result, many benefits were achieved, such as his and her bathrooms in the master suite and north and south balconies. The views over the East River through large windows that face north, east, and south are stunning from anywhere in the apartment. The clients felt that the previous owner's architecture suited the design direction.

Keogh's approach was to bring the colors from the world outside to inside the apartment. The large expanse of the sky, the green waters of the East River, and the morning sunrises gave an easy direction of palette colors for the space. She took advantage of the varying ceiling heights by emphasizing the highest areas with sky blue metallic paint, creating a floating effect, and bringing the sky into the apartment.

The client wanted an elegant, sophisticated Manhattan feel. The best part was that Ms. Keogh could literally think up any design, any finish, or color (that they all agreed upon), and the clients, who are experts in custom furniture, would be building most of the custom furniture. A rare opportunity!

A wooden and silk gridded piece of furniture was made as a focal point of the entry, using a beveled mirror to widen the narrow space further.

Courtesy of Dan Muro.

The blue silk carries the blue from the ceiling and has the same reflective value. Ms. Keogh carried this gridded theme subtly through the rest of the apartment, on the folding screen in the living room, the partitioned coffee table, in the bar area, in the gridded sections of the den cabinetry, and the subtle "shoji" grid in the office.

Two large columns that carry ductwork for the building hindered the visual impact of the entry foyer. Ms. Keogh mirrored each inner side to "open" the space.

The living room had a raised ceiling, dividing the right and left hand sides of the room. The bar area to the right was to stay, and the clients decided to use the center raised ceiling and stone floor area for a combina- tion foyer and dining table. The space by the bar was turned into an informal living room. The other larger space became the more formal elegant living room. The existing bronze mirrors were great in that they reflected the view but were too modern for the Hovivians' taste. To lessen their impact, Ms. Keogh incorporated drapery and a custom glass folding screen.

Four columns of wood were built, unifying both sides of the room. These columns are actually storage cabi- nets for dinner and glassware for the dining room. The shimmery draperies twinkle like the lights on the city.

The clients collected the Buddhas and boat through their extensive travels. The artwork in the foyer is a com- missioned piece by Donna Oehmig.

Courtesy of Dan Muro.

Courtesy of Dan Muro.

216

The kitchen and family room is to the right off the entry foyer. The storage space in their new kitchen exceeds that of their previous suburban home through a design that utilized every inch of space. A double pull-out pantry holds large quantities of food. The light maple wood cabinets expand the feeling of space in this compact kitchen. Soft, cool green tones with light maple kept the office/guest room very simple. A modern version of a shoji sliding panel cabinet achieved maximum storage.

The space between the kitchen and den was so deep that Ms. Keogh was able to add more storage on the den side. The den steps down from the kitchen; consequently, the storage in the kitchen becomes a "wood" wall to the breakfast eating area.

The den was a narrow room with spectacular views. Ms. Keogh chose to angle the sofa to create a long view to the window. The shallow cabinetry held a flat screen TV. Ms. Keogh also wanted the shelves and storage to appear to float, so that they are anchored invisibly. To marry the kitchen and den together, the light maple wood of the kitchen was incorporated into the den, with a cherry veneer brought in for warmth.

Courtesy of Dan Muro.

Courtesy of Dan Muro.

Courtesy of Dan Muro.

The master bedroom is a total retreat to the world outside. The green aqua color of the fabric-paneled walls brings in the water and sky. The warm wooden furniture brings a clean traditional feel to the room. A beautiful chaise provides a quiet place to read and reflect.

The woodland scene painting is by Charles Yoder.

Courtesy of Dan Muro.

APPENDIX: ARCHITECTS, DESIGNERS, & OTHERS

Lavae Aldrich is a principal of **Aldrich Architects**, founded in 1988 and based in Issaquah, Washington. She concentrates on residential design for new construction and remodeling. About half of the firm's work is transitional housing and emergency shelters. With a branch office in Costa Rica, Lavae designs vacation/retirement homes that are eco-friendly and suited to the climate.

28 Front St. N., Issaquah, WA 98027
425.391.5308
lavae@aldricharchitects.com;
www.aldricharchitects.com

American Ingenuity manufactures the dome shell kit, which is shipped to the construction site. It has dome houses in forty-seven states and seven foreign areas. The building kit consists of the component panels needed for the assembly on the dome shell. The panels contain all the insulation, interior wallboard, and about eighty percent of the finished steel reinforced concrete exterior. All doors, window, and interior items are purchased locally. A super strong, energy-efficient, low maintenance dome home can be finished turn key for about the same price per square foot as a conventional house.

8777 Holiday Springs Rd., Rockledge, FL 32955
321.639.8777
info@aidomes.com; www.aidomes.com

Next generation architecture describes the innovative architectural firm of **Avila Design**. The firm believes that the twenty-first century must signal a renewed design approach while paying respect to the past. It specializes in unique solutions to residential, retail, and commercial projects with its practice built on thoughtful and uncompromising dedication to design excellence.

436 14th St. Suite 1123, Oakland, CA 94612
510.893.2000
www.aviladesign.com

The primary goal of **Sears Barrett Architects** as residential architects is to discover and give form to the unique aspirations of its clients. The firm's design-oriented approach encourages client collaboration in shaping dwellings that benefit the land and the client. It believes that an artfully crafted residence can contribute directly to their clients' experience of living well.

7901 East Belleview Ave., Suite 250
Englewood, CO 80111
303.804.0688
info@searsbarrett.com; www.searsbarrett.com

Victoria Benatar (Urban) is a registered architect (AIA-CAV) and the principal of her own internationally recognized award-winning firm in New York City. She develops architecture, interior design, and digital and urban design projects worldwide. She was an adjunct assistant professor at the Columbia University Graduate School of Architecture, Planning, and Preservation and works as a part-time faculty at Parsons School of Design.

257 E 61 St. #4E New York, NY 10021
212.755.0525
vbu@e-arquitectura.com; www.e-arquitectura.com

Design Northwest Architects, Inc., is one of the Northwest region's leading architecture, urban design, and planning firms. Established in 1990, the firm is recognized for its innovative exploration of design and its wide range of experience in complex building types for residential, commercial, and institutional use. The firm builds on the real needs of their clients, with a keen eye on the context of each site's surroundings. Principals and associates are renowned for bringing each commission a fresh spirit, celebrating its distinctive characteristics, and enhancing the experience of daily living, working, and playing.

10031 SR 532, Suite B, Stanwood, WA 98292
360.629.3441
info@designsnw.com; www.designsnw.com

Prior to launching her own practice, **Anne-Sophie Divenyi** worked for offices on both coasts and in Basel, Switzerland, where she worked for Diener + Diener Architekten. In the Boston area, she has worked with William Rawn Associates, where she oversaw Northeastern University's award-winning West Campus Village Residence Halls and the Center for Theatre and Dance for Williams College. Ms. Divenyi is currently a lead designer at Ann Beha Architects. She has taught at Rice University, the Boston Architectural Center, and in Harvard's Career Discovery Program prior to joining the Northeastern faculty as an adjunct professor, where she teaches design studio and architectural history.

33 Kingston Street, Boston, MA 02111
617.338.3000
adivenyi@annbeha.com; www.annbeha.com

Tony Fallon of **Tony Fallon Architecture** says, "Architecture is the act of composing the built environment. The palette with which we work is full of possibilities and requirements encompassing the needs and wishes of the client. While many make do with the checker cab approach of compilation, architects design places to achieve a beautiful, workable, and durable environment. Our firm's ability and mission is to make you look good, make your life easier, and to help you have fun in the procurement of an enjoyable building or building project."

501 Barn Door Gap
Strafford, NH 03884-6233
603.269.3206
aeropera@worldpath.net; www.fallon.fly.to

Mark Farber Design, based in Orleans, Massachusetts, has over twenty-five years' experience in both design and hands-on construction work, primarily in the renovation, remodeling, and the adaptive reuse of buildings. The firm prides itself on its ability to integrate the present-day functional needs of any client program into the buildings it is asked to reuse and expand. Specializing in working with old structures, the firm has worked on such diverse projects as a child's playhouse to urban row houses to residential estates.

59 Finlay Rd., Orleans, MA 02653
508.240.3242 or 410.591.0534
mdfarber@earthlink.net

Located in Almaden Valley and established in 1983, **Debra Kay George Interiors** offers a complete design service. Ms. George is particularly adept when it comes to new construction projects, where she is involved at the architectural phase. With her space-planning talent, construction knowledge, creativity, and eye for color, she coordinates the project from the beginning, specifying the interior detailing, layout, furnishings, and finishes – transforming concept to reality. A professional member and past vice president of IDG and Allied Member of ASID, she has participated in many showcase homes and been featured in many publications.

65874 Camden Ave., San Jose, CA 95120
408.997.1143
debrakg@pacbell.net;
www.debrakaygeorgeinteriors.com

Charlene Keogh, the owner of **Keogh Design Inc.,** has been practicing interior design for twenty-nine years. She has interior design projects throughout the United States and received AIA's Excellence in Interiors award. *Interior Design, Design Times,* and *Dwell* magazines have published her projects. Her work also includes numerous furniture and product designs for individual clients.

180 Duane St. 2nd floor, New York, NY 10013
212.964.4170
ck@keoghdesign.com; www.keoghdesign.com

Alan Mascord Design Associates, a Portland, Oregon, architectural design firm was founded in 1983. Known throughout the industry for successful solutions to many difficult building programs and, not restricted to any one particular architectural style, its creative staff is renowned for beautiful, unique, and efficient home designs. Not only does the firm have hundreds of proven home plans available, its team of designers is available to either modify one of the existing plans or create a "custom" design from scratch.

1305 NW 18th Ave., Portland, OR 97209
800.411.0231 or 503.225.9161
1300 SW 7th Street, Suite 104, Renton, WA 98055
866.512.1157 or 425.277.7501
www.mascord.com

Rupinder Singh, the owner of **Mimar Design**, is a Boston-based architect with an interest in creating visually clean yet tectonically and materially lavish environments for the residential and commercial client. His design solutions are an integration of aesthetic pleasure, functionality, and durability.

21 Shepard St., #34, Cambridge, MA 02138
617.669.4352
mimardesign@hotmail.com
www.mimardesign.com

Moskow Architects, Inc., is a Boston-based firm offering professional services in architecture, urban design, landscape architecture, and interior design. In practice since 1990, the firm has planned and designed a variety of buildings, including office and retail facilities, institutional buildings, and custom residences, as well as master plans for future growth and strategic development in urban areas. The firm, which specializes in sustainable, environmentally sensitive architecture, has received national and regional awards for design excellence.

88 Broad St., Boston, MA 02110
617.292.2000
km@moskowarchitects.com;
www.MoskowArchitects.com

Penn National Golf Course Community features a community where an affordable, outstanding lifestyle meets a great location. Penn National is just ninety miles from Washington, DC, Virginia, and Maryland. Penn National offers the finest in golf course living, with every comfort and amenity you could wish for close at hand. It offers custom homes with breathtaking mountain views and natural landscapes, to easy-care town homes and villas built on lovely fairways.

3720 Clubhouse Drive, Fayetteville, PA 17222
800.338.523
www.pennhomes.com

Campion A. Platt Architect, PC is a full service architecture and interior design practice, which specializes in highly custom residential and commercial design, interior design, and interior furnishings for private, commercial, and institutional clients. With a holistic approach and an appreciation for a wide variety of worldly architectural styles, its founder Campion Platt is known for creating soothing spaces and interiors awash with contrasting textures provided by the built-in architecture, furniture, and art.

152 Madison Ave., Suite 900, New York, NY 10016
212 .779.3835
www.campionplatt.com

E.R. Racek Associates is a full-service architectural firm. Since 1977, it has been involved with a variety of projects, including both new construction and renovation work for the public as well as the private sector. Its staff has a wide range of capabilities – from designing high-rise office buildings and condominium developments to restoring historic buildings, solving space problems, and designing additions.

180 Canal St., Boston, MA 02114
617.367.0785
er.racek@verizon.net; www.erracek.com

Rodwin Architecture is a small, award-winning full service firm located in Boulder, Colorado. The firm specializes in sustainable custom houses, offering architectural, interior, and landscape design services as well as planning, feasibility, marketing, construction management, and development assistance. Experienced in both residential and commercial projects of all sizes throughout the country, it is known for award-winning designs, friendly, responsive service, and expertise in the arena of sustainable "green" design. It is particularly known for its work on straw bale houses.

1425 Pearl St., Suite B, Boulder, CO 80302
303.413.8556
info@rodwinarch.com; www.rodwinarch.com

Sabre Yachts Corporation has been hand crafting high quality luxury sailboats and motor yachts since 1971. Built to NMMA, ABYC standards and CE certified, its boats combine cutting-edge design and fabrication with skills derived from the boat building tradition that has been alive in Maine since the nineteenth century.

Hawthorne Rd., Box 134 South Casco, ME 04077
207.655.3831
sabre@sabreyachts.com; www.sabreyachts.com

Terrasol Restoration & Renovation Co. (from the Latin for *earth* and *sun*) has been in business since 1988. The firm focuses on four categories: restoration, renovation, new "green" construction, and historic log structures. In every category, materials are recycled, reused, and dedicated to extending life spans and preserving historic value. Terrasol's projects range from small remodeling jobs to architecturally designed new and renovated homes to structures listed on the National Register of Historic Places.

300 S. Minnesota Ave., St. Peter, MN 56082
507.934.1818
info@terrasol.net; www.terrasol.net

Thielsen Architects, Inc. P.S. is a vibrant design-oriented firm that is committed to creating distinctive environments. It believes that thoughtful spatial organization and sensitivity to the site and natural light achieve sensible design solutions. The firm strives to design architecture that will remain as functional and beautiful over time as it is today.

720 Market St., Suite C, Kirkland, WA 98033
425.828.0333
inquiries@thielsen.com
www.thielsenarchitects.com

Topsider Homes are designed for waterfront living with plenty of deck space, vaulted, exposed-beam ceilings, and breathtaking panoramic views throughout. A unique pedestal design also makes an ideal alternative to coastal area pilings and provides the perfect building solution for severely sloping lakefront sites.

P.O. Box 1490, Clemmons, NC 27012
866.867.9300 or 336.766.9300
topsider@topsider.com; www.topsider.com

Sandra Vitzthum Architect LLC creates settings for meaningful public and private life by celebrating craftsmanship, the human spirit, and our connections to family, community, place, and nature. Founded in 1994, her firm specializes in traditional and ecologically sound design. About two-thirds of her practice is residential, and one-third is civic or commercial. Although most of her work is architectural, she also does village planning, landscape, and furniture design.

46 East State Street, Montpelier, VT 05602
802.223.1806
mail@sandravitzthum.com; www.sandravitzthum.com

Kristi Woloszyn, AIA is a registered architect currently residing in Wells, Maine, and working at Gawron Turgeon Architects. Her experience derives from years of designing homes in varying climates such as Southern Florida, Central Arizona, New Mexico, and now New England. Her mixture of cultural influences produces an exciting and innovative style.

29 Black Point Rd., Scarborough, ME 04074
207.883.6307
kwoloszyn@gawronturgeon.co; www.gawron.com

Since 1969, **Yankee Barn Homes** has been designing and building post and beam homes. Working with one of the firm's designers, homeowners create a unique Yankee Barn to fit their lifestyle and site. Each home is then built from the finest materials one at a time in the protected, controlled environment of the firm's workshop. The Yankee Barn home is raised on site and enclosed (usually in less than seven days). Inside the weather tight shell of a Yankee Barn home, the builder can finish the home.

131 Yankee Barn Rd. Grantham, NH 03753
800.258.9786
www.yankeebarnhomes.com

National Association of Home Builders (NAHB) is a trade association that helps promote the policies that make housing a national priority. Since 1942, NAHB has been serving its members, the housing industry, and the public at large. For over forty years, NAHB has been the nation's leading source for housing information. Chances are if you need to learn more about a specific area of home building, NAHB has a publication for you.

1201 15th Street, NW
Washington, DC 20005
202-266-8200 x 0
800-368-5242
www.www.homebuilder.com

Helen Pape is a realtor in Venice, Florida. Currently, she works with Michael Saunders and Company, who handles properties in all price ranges. The firm specializes in high-end properties.

941.223.1457.
helenpape@michaelsaunders.com
www.michaelsaunders.com

INDEX